Eat the Elephants and Fight the Ants

How to Take More Control of Your Time

Tom McConalogue

BLACKHALL
Publishing

This book was typeset by Artwerk for

BLACKHALL PUBLISHING
27 Carysfort Avenue
Blackrock
Co. Dublin
Ireland

e-mail: blackhall@eircom.net

ISBN: 1 842180 47 9

© Tom McConalogue, 1999, 2003

First Published 1999
Second Edition 2003

A catalogue record for this book is available from the British Library.

Printed in Ireland by
ColourBooks Ltd.

Eat the Elephants and Fight the Ants

How to Take More Control of Your Time

About the Author

As an independent consultant in the areas of management and organisation development, Tom also teaches at the Irish Management Institute where he runs management training programmes including time management. He has wide experience in the private and public sectors and has worked on many overseas training and consulting assignments in Europe, the Middle and Far East, and the United States.

In the early part of his career, Tom worked in the personnel, training and organisation development functions of several major companies. He completed his Masters Degree in organisation development (OD) at Pepperdine University in Los Angeles and his Doctorate in the management of change at Bath University.

Tom's interests include working as a process consultant with companies that are managing their own transitions. He also has an ongoing interest in helping managers improve their personal and interpersonal skills. Currently he divides his time between consulting, teaching and writing.

Contents

Introduction

Over the past decade time has become a much more difficult and complex resource to manage, for two reasons. Firstly the environment in which we work has changed – while customers want instant response, and staff and colleagues are making more demands on our time, managers are also being challenged to radically improve service, teamwork, quality, delivery and costs. All this has put pressure on people to work longer and faster to keep up with the increasing demands on their time, estimated by one survey as an additional month's work a year over the last twenty years.

Secondly, time is becoming a more difficult resource to control because of the way managers respond to the operational demands in their day. While the growth in office technology and information systems has helped to speed up the workflow it has also encouraged managers to become better organised around the wrong things. By definition, managing is not just about getting things done for today, it is also about doing things today to ensure the future; about being proactive as well as reactive, strategic as well as operational. But with their attention and focus on what has to be done for today, or this week, it is all too easy for managers to end up doing things right instead of doing the right things.

> Efficiency is doing things right
> Effectiveness is doing the right things
> Excellence is doing the right things right

One of the major challenges for managers today is how to make time for the bigger and more important things in the job when there are so many small things demanding their immediate attention. We all recognise the ELEPHANTS in our lives that we find so hard to manage, whether starting projects, tackling a paperwork backlog, losing weight or getting down to study. Remember the tale of the five blind men feeling their way around an elephant, each having a different idea of what the elephant looked like? Not only are the bigger things harder to visualise but they are difficult to start and to keep energy for over the long haul; as Rosabeth Moss Kanter once suggested "all projects look like a failure half way through". Yet for many of us it is the bigger and more abstract things that are the real challenges in the job and the most important source of reward in our personal lives.

And apart from the elephants there is also a constant stream of ANTS in the day – the minor derailments that we do not even notice eating into what we are trying to get done. While they may only take a few minutes here or there, cumulatively they can add up to a great deal of time – and more damaging than their immediate effect is that they often take our focus away from the important things in the day. But, like the ticks and the termites that irritate elephants, we get used to distractions and interruptions in our day, even enjoy their company, and would miss them if they were gone. While the ants may block us from making progress on the important things, in the same way as an old car or a bad relationship, it is hard to let go of familiar things even when they are preventing us from getting what we want in our jobs or our personal lives.

The ELEPHANTS and ANTS serve to illustrate the many complexities and competing demands on our time. Making the space and energy to do the things that you really *want* to get done while dealing with the things you *have* to get done is more complex than many of the popular remedies suggest – as Sweigers Law counsels, "for every large and enormously complex problem there is a quick and simple solution – and it is always wrong". More important than looking for better ways to organise your busyness or to speed up the workflow is starting to make wiser choices, recognising that it isn't a question of elephants or ants but getting the right balance, so you don't lose sight of the important things, or your flexibility to the immediate opportunities and to the fun there is in managing.

Managing Time is about taking more control of what is less and less controllable

Chapter 1

Making Better Choices with Time

Being effective as a manager is about making good choices with your time. Most of the problems that managers have with time are the result of having many things to do and a limited amount of time in which to do them. So they have to make choices about which activities add most to their effectiveness and put the time where it belongs.

Managing time also means choosing to do some things now and leaving other things until later, identifying some things as important and others as less important, and acknowledging that some things are worth giving less of your time or none at all. But making those sometimes difficult and confusing decisions also creates stress – life was indeed simpler and less stressful when you had two pairs of shoes or one breakfast cereal to choose from.

BAD HABITS AND STRESS

Under pressure from the many competing demands on their time, some managers avoid the stress that goes with making difficult choices by developing habits that are self-defeating and difficult to reverse. Managers typically get into four bad habits with time.

Trying to Do Everything

One of the ways in which managers attempt to cope with the increasing pressures in the job is by extending their day – coming in early, leaving late, grabbing a hurried lunch and taking work home in their briefcase. A recent report by the Institute of Management found over 38 per cent of managers working more than 50 hours a week and 41 per cent regularly taking work home at the weekends.

Not only does working long hours become a habit (many managers would not know what to do with themselves if they went home on time), it is also a vain attempt to get everything done. The well-established principle in Parkinson's Law that "work expands to fill the available time", should remind us that no matter how many hours you have in the day there will never be enough time to get everything done. Working long hours to beat your way out of over commitment and time pressure is not very skilful – any old fool can work hard – but neither is it managing, it is being managed!

Focusing on Urgency

A second habit that managers develop in an attempt to get more control of their time, is to favour urgency over importance. In the typical working day, many things are urgent but only a few things are really that important. God forbid, if any one of us were knocked down in the road tomorrow, most of what we do would be picked up by somebody else or might not get done at all with very little consequence. It supports a view that the manager's contribution to the organisation lies in the few important things they achieve in their day, not in the volume of routine work and urgency they handle. But in the typical working day the important things often get done last rather than first, or are completed outside working hours when managers have least energy for thinking or planning.

Focusing on the immediate and urgent tasks sees many managers drifting effortlessly into the "activity trap" where crisis and reaction dictate the workload rather than being driven by the manager's own aspirations and challenges in the job.

Hanging on to the Routine

A third habit that managers develop under pressure from time is retreating into routine work. Daily correspondence, reports, paperwork and appointments are examples of the kind of work that managers are only too willing to commit their time without thinking about the contribution it is making to their effectiveness. Many managers spend the first and most important hour of their day on tasks that may be necessary but are also part of the comfort zone, like opening the post, checking e-mails, responding to telephone messages or following up on post-it notes. Don't you enjoy getting back to the office after a holiday or business trip to find an assortment of messages, e-mail and post-it notes to relax you into the first couple of hours? Be honest.

Much of the routine work in the manager's day is at best work they should be giving to others, work they should be giving less time or work they should not be doing at all. Yet managers continue to occupy themselves with a great deal of routine and trivia in their day either because it is familiar work they do not want to let go of, or because it serves as a convenient alibi for not getting into the more challenging and difficult parts of the job.

Saying "Yes" instead of "No"

How often have you come away from a meeting only to kick yourself for having said "yes" to something. Over 70 per cent of managers admit to saying "yes" too often and recognise in themselves the need to be more assertive with their time.

Saying "yes" when you should be saying "no" is a habit that comes from two sources. Under pressure it is often easier to say "yes" to things, particularly if they are somewhere in the future. If a colleague asked you to do something in three weeks time you would probably say "yes", while if the same colleague asked you to drop everything right now and give them an hour of your time your answer would probably be more thoughtful.

Saying "yes" to things when you should be saying "no" is also a product of not having clear direction in your own job. If you do not have clear priorities to which you are committing chunks of time in your day it is much more difficult to say "no" to the demands of others. Alternatively, if you are committed to getting a major report completed in the next two days it is much easier to say "no" to people. And saying "no" does not mean turning down every request, but it does mean making choices that are based on the effective use of your time and not regretting the sometimes ill-considered decisions that contribute to wasting time.

Figure 1.1: Symptoms and Bad Habits

Rate the following symptoms or habits as:
a big problem – 2, problem – 1, no problem – 0

1. Working long hours or taking work home.

2. Feeling of overwork or pressure in the job.

3. Always urgency and crises in the job.

4. Not giving enough time to the major priorities.

5. Too much time spent on paperwork and routine administration.

6. Doing routine work that could be done by others.

7. Not saying "no" often enough.

8. Responding to many demands from customers, colleagues or staff.

Add your marks:

1 – 2 Doing too much.

3 – 4 Focusing on urgency.

5 – 6 Hanging on to the routine.

7 – 8 Saying "yes" too often.

Many of the work habits that managers develop as a way of coping with time pressures in the job are self-defeating in the short term and habitual in the longer term. And, like most bad habits, they are hard to break because managers get comfortable with working long hours, responding to urgency and over committing themselves to others. While some managers grudgingly admit to being stressed and overworked, many have an investment in their illness as well as in the cure because it allows them to justify their ineffectiveness to themselves and attracts sympathy from others. But ask yourself this: "To what degree are my time problems caused by the demands of the job, or have I just drifted into working this way?" While there are some things that managers have little option but to get done, much of the way they use their time is guided by habit or by choice. Recognising where you have control and what you can do nothing about is an important step in making better choices.

> *God, grant me the serenity to accept*
> *the things I cannot change,*
>
> *The courage to change the things I can,*
>
> *And the wisdom to know the difference.*

MAKING BETTER CHOICES

Although time is like any other resource in the job, such as money, people or equipment, it is a difficult resource to manage and an almost impossible one to control. Not only is it totally perishable (you cannot save an hour today and use it tomorrow when you are busy) but time is always in short supply. If you reduced the number of hours available to you in your working day by the amount of time you spend on minor issues, on things to which you should have said "no", on work you should have given to others and the time you waste on interruptions and distractions, then you are left with no more than two or three really productive hours in the average day. Respected commentators, like Peter Drucker, Edward Demming and Gareth Morgan, all agree that managers have less than 25 per cent of their time under their control. The only way to use those precious hours wisely is to ensure that your choices are guided by what you want to get done rather than letting events and other people make those choices for you.

Habit 1: Know Where the Hours are Going

The place to start managing yourself is not with what you want to do in the future but how you are using your time right now. Most managers over and underestimate the amount of time they give to their major tasks by at least 50 per cent, and most people could not give a decent account of how they spent yesterday, never mind last week. The shortage of data on where their time actually goes is a major block to managers who want to make better and more informed choices for the future.

Habit 2: Keep the End in Mind

As one adage predicts: "If you do not know where you are going, you may end up somewhere else." By definition, managing is not just about doing things for today, it is also about changing things, improving things and developing things for the future.

While most managers have an appreciation of their strategic function, they also find it remarkably easy to fill up their day with activities that have little to do with managing the future. And, as a manager, apart from finding your own sense of direction in the job, it is much easier to get others to share the journey if they too are inspired by your hopes and dreams for the future.

Habit 3: Work to Priorities

Many managers end up giving away their effectiveness by assuming that everything they do is of equal importance. Yet ask any manager to list their key tasks in the job and few have any problem identifying the four or five activities that stand out above the rest.

While it almost goes without saying that having priorities is a good thing, the main issue is finding time to manage them. Many managers who have clear and challenging priorities end up giving very little of their time to them – less than 10 per cent according to Henry Mintzberg in *The Nature of Managerial Work*. Apart from having longer term priorities to provide you with a sense of direction, it is also important to find disciplines for working on them daily and weekly to ensure that you focus on the things you want to make happen as well as the things that you need to get done.

Habit 4: Schedule Time for the Important Things

Priorities are a function of what you pay attention to, by giving them time. If you say that something is a priority and you are not giving it solid chunks of your day or week, then by definition it is not a priority. Likewise, most important and big things get done if you make time for them, like developing relationships, passing exams or getting fit. While it is easy for managers to excuse their lack of achievement by saying "I didn't have the time" or "I have been working under pressure", like most people they can always find time for things they really want to do, like attending an overseas conference or a golf outing. The way you commit to your priorities is by making time for them, whether by blocking out hours in your diary, using a "to do" list or institutionalising them as regular commitments for particular hours of the day or specific days of the week.

Habit 5: Delegate Routine and Responsibility

Making more time for the important things in your job also means letting go some of the less important things, either by getting your staff more involved in handling the routine work, developing procedures for handling recurring problems, or empowering your staff to take more risks, make mistakes, and learn from them. Most managers could also let go of an amount of their paperwork, meetings or queries by giving them less of their time or by pushing them back to those who should be dealing with them in the first place. Adopting the habit of dealing with the most important tasks first thing in the morning is also a way of relegating the least important things to times of the day where many of them belong.

Habit 6: Confront your Indecision and Delay

No matter how committed they may be to the important tasks in their day, most people procrastinate on certain things, whether finishing a report, completing staff appraisals or dealing with a problem person. While they are sometimes positive reactions to things we are not sure about, procrastination and indecision can also become bad habits when managers, through fear of failure, do not start them at all or wait for a crisis to spur them into action. Confronting the anxiety that accompanies indecision and procrastination means finding ways to see them as manageable challenges rather than as opportunities to fail.

Habit 7: Get the Best out of your Boss

While many of the daily distractions in the manager's day come from below, they are also subjected to many influences from above. Not only can bosses and colleagues add a great deal of distraction to what you are trying to do by shifting priorities or setting unrealistic deadlines, but managers also have to work with peers and bosses to get the results they are trying to achieve.

Managing upwards means finding the right approaches and quality time to network with and influence colleagues and bosses who may be in a position to support or block your progress as a manager. In the same way as other relationships, it means understanding them as people, keeping them informed, making time for them and being assertive in ways that deepen rather than undermine the relationship.

Habit 8: Minimise the Daily Distractions

The typical manager's day is fragmented by interruption from the telephone, visitors, minor problems and *ad hoc* meetings. While they may only take a few minutes here and there, the cumulative effect of time wasters can add up to a massive block to getting things done. And though you may not be able to get rid of time wasters altogether, because many of them go with the job, you could start to manage the effects of interruption on your day by recognising the extent to which you collude or even encourage the things about which you complain. Enjoy some time wasters for what they are, part of the buzz of the job, and find ways to manage others by minimising them or controlling their effect on getting the important things done.

Habit 9: De-stress the Work Pressure

While there is nothing wrong with the kind of stress that accompanies a tight deadline or a crisis, it is the negative side of work pressure that managers recognise in themselves. Many of the habits that managers develop to cope with the effects of work pressure, such as long hours, coffee, cigarettes or self-medication, simply add to symptoms, such as anxiety interrupted sleep, lack of concentration and digestive problems.

Two broad approaches to stress management emphasise firstly, the importance of building time into your day for relaxation, on the basis that managing is a stressful activity, and, secondly, in the longer term, by developing habits to reduce or eliminate the root causes of stress.

Habit 10: Start to Make it Happen

Many responses to time pressure are developed in a manager's early career when he or she is striving for recognition and promotion and learning from the bad habits of others. Although some habits serve a function in dealing with short-term crises and urgency, they frequently persist well beyond their usefulness and only in later career do managers regret how much time they gave to some things and how little to others. How many managers will end up regretting that they did not take enough care of their health or spend more time with their families? How many will recognise their long hours as having blocked them from achieving other things with their lives? And how many on their deathbeds will regret that they did not spend enough time in the office?

Managing time means accepting that you have little choice about doing some things, but that many others are within your control. As well as looking for better ways to organise your "busyness", start to challenge some of the behaviours that may be getting in the way of what you really want to achieve with your time. Learn to unblock the bad habits that may be sustaining an unhealthy work style or preventing you from getting more satisfaction from managing. Find ways to get more mileage from your efforts by focusing on the things you really want to make happen and scheduling time for them. Do something to let go of one of your major time wasters or get more balance in your personal life. If you do not start managing your time it can easily end up controlling you.

ELEPHANTS & ANTS

Everyone ends up being busy, the question is "busy doing what?" While there are some things that we have to do as part of the job, many others are a choice. It is important to recognise that many of the bad work habits that we fall into are ways of avoiding difficult choices with our time, such as trying to do everything, focusing on urgency at the expense of the important things, retreating into the comfort zone of routine work and saying "yes" to things when we should be saying "no".

Resolve to start making wiser choices with your time by committing to the real challenges in the job and letting go some of the urgency and routine that can so easily fill your day and contribute little to your effectiveness.

You will never have time
for everything
And yet you have all the time
there is

Chapter 2

Know where the Hours are Going

When managers first begin to experience problems with time, their immediate response is to look for a handy panacea, whether a new diary, a personal organiser, a resolution to start working differently or a demand for additional staff. Isn't that one of the reasons you bought this book – to look for solutions?

Imagine, however, that you had a weight problem and went along to a fitness centre for help. Would they start by telling you to go on a crash diet, follow their exercise plan or cut out certain foods? No, they would probably begin by giving you a fitness test, weighing you or enquiring about your current diet. They know that the way you start changing habits is not with solutions but with data. Understanding what is happening in your life and the options for doing things differently is the key to changing most things for the future.

One of the major obstacles to changing our habits with time is that people do not have even the most basic of data on where their time actually goes. Most managers could not give a decent account of how they spent yesterday and few would have more than a hazy idea of what they did last week. Added to that, managers, like most people, are poor judges of time, underestimating the hours they need to get most things done by at least 50 per cent, never budgeting enough time for the important tasks and assuming that their staff can do things in half the time required. It should be of real concern today that many businesses which profess to have such tight controls on their other resources, such as materials, money and equipment, have so little information on what their managers and staff are doing with their time.

THE "BUSYNESS" TRAP

Like most people, managers are poor judges of time because their experience relates to what they are doing – time speeds up when you are doing things you enjoy and slows down when you are doing things you dislike. Attempting to simplify the theory of relativity, Albert Einstein once suggested that it was like "being in the company of a beautiful woman for a minute of time and sitting on top of a red hot fire for the same length of time – it's a different experience". Although we measure time as if it were a constant, in reality it speeds up and slows down as we go through the day.

> With the aid of a timer or watch, and sitting in a comfortable position, try to judge a minute of time. Resist the temptation to start counting, just try to feel the minute. When you think the minute is up, check the timer and see how far your estimate is out. Most people under or overestimate a minute by at least fifteen seconds.

Confused about where their time is going, except that they are not getting enough mileage from all the hours they are putting into the job is an inducement for many managers to work even harder to beat their way out of over commitment and under achievement. Rather than looking at what they are doing with their time, managers often retreat into "busyness" and overwork on the basis that if you do not know where you are going at least you can look good. Unfortunately, for many managers, looking good means drifting into habits that are hard to break, such as long hours, taking work home and an over concern for the routine and the trivia.

Managing time is not about getting more things done in the day; it is a process for finding ways to focus on the important things while at the same time avoiding the activity trap. And the place to start the process is with looking at where your time is going as a guide to where it should go for the future.

While there are simple ways to account for your time on a daily or weekly basis, it is useful now and again to carry out a more thoughtful review by keeping a log, reviewing your diary or touching base with your feelings and frustrations about time.

Keep a Time Log

A periodic review of your time does not have to be a complicated exercise, but if you feel under constant pressure or are getting less than you expect from the hours you are putting into the job, then consider keeping a simple record over a couple of typical working days.

Figure 2.1: Time Log

		P.	D.	W.	O/M
8.30–8.45	Checking daily work	✓			M
8.45–9.00	Opening post		✓		O
9.00–9.15	Answering correspondence		✓	✓	O
9.15–9.30	Responding to queries		✓		O
9.30–9.45	Responding to queries		✓	✓	O
9.45–10.00	Production meeting			✓	M
10.00–10.15	Production meeting			✓	O
10.15–10.30	Production meeting	✓			O
10.30–10.45	MBWA	✓			M
10.45–11.00	Meeting John re invoice		✓		O
		30%	50%	40%	30%

Start by taking a sheet of lined paper and identify each line as a quarter hour in your working day. Over the next day or two, write down what you are doing in each quarter hour as you are doing it. Complete the record as close to the time as possible and do not leave it beyond an hour. When you get to the end of the day, add up the total number of quarter hours you worked on that day.

Now analyse the data under four simple headings.

1. **Priorities**. In the first column go down through the activities for each quarter hour and identify which were priorities on that day – priorities are tasks that made a significant contribution to what you were trying to achieve, not the things that had to be done or took a lot of your time. Be ruthless in identifying the real priorities; they are by definition a few rather than many things. Now add up the number of quarter hours you spent on priority activities that day and percentage it over the total number of quarter hours available.

2. **Delegation**. In the second column, again go down the list for each quarter hour and identify the delegatable activities – those tasks you could or should have given to someone else to complete – including the priority activities. You may find that although you could not delegate a whole task you could have given part of it to someone else.

As well as the tasks you could have given to others, also consider tasks you could have let go by saying "no" or giving less of your time to. Now add up the number of quarter hours you spent on *D*s and percentage it over the total.

3. **Time Wasters**. Next, go down through the list and identify the time you spent dealing with interruptions and distractions on that day. Include the things that took you from what you were trying to get done or the tasks to which you should have said "no". Time wasters are sometimes difficult to identify because many of them are part of the job; it is only when they eat into the major activities or start to affect your ability to manage the day that they become a problem. Again, add up the number of *W*s and percentage it over the total.

4. **Operating and Managing**. In the final column go down through the list of activities and identify them as managing or operating work – put an *O* or an *M* beside each quarter hour. Although there is an element of greyness between managing and operating work, *managing* activities are those which relate to "achieving results through other people", such as planning, delegation or reviewing results. Conversely, *operating* tasks are the technical/professional part of your job or the routine work which could be done by others. Again add up the time you spent on operating and managing work that day and calculate the percentage balance.

Having completed the analysis ask yourself a few questions or, better still, write half a page of commentary to yourself.

• What kind of day was it: effective or busy?
• What was good or disappointing about the way you spent your time on that day?
• How typical was it of your normal working day?
• What is the data telling you about the way in which you currently use your time and could use it better?

Keeping a time log over a couple of typical working days is always revealing, sometimes reassuring and often disturbing. Managers who keep a log are usually surprised at how little time they spend on the priorities and how their priorities get side-tracked by the volume of routine work or urgent tasks in their day. Also revealing is that much of the work on which managers spend their time could be delegated to others if they gave more consideration to clarifying people's jobs and allocated real responsibility to their key staff. And, typically, an average of 20 per cent of the manager's day is wasted by distractions, which fragment their day and eat into their major priorities.

Figure 2.2: Key Task Analysis

Tasks	M	T	W	T	F	Tot

A simpler version of the time log involves listing the 6–8 key tasks in your job and tracking the time you give them over the next week, indicating in hours or parts of an hour how much time you spend on each activity per day. The simple action of tracking your time on the important activities is often enough to start changing them.

Review your Diary

One record of where managers commit their time is a diary. While diaries can be a useful tool in scheduling for the future, they are also part of the time trap for managers who frequently use them to record commitments they should never have agreed in the first place. Managers also get some comfort from having a full diary, which relieves them from having to do anything except religiously follow their diary commitments. Not only do managers tend to commit time to others at the expense of their own priorities but a full diary is often used as an excuse for their lack of effectiveness in the day.

One of the ways to get data on how much time is spent on specific activities, such as meetings, visits, travel, presentations, networking or appointments, is to analyse the last three to six months of your diary. Use the analysis to identify the tasks that take up a lot of your time and those for which you may need to schedule more time.

As Director of service in a healthcare organisation, Alan spends a great deal of his time at meetings, some regular and some *ad hoc*, some internal and others with outside agencies. The feeling that he was just rushing from one meeting to another prompted him to count up the hours he spent at meetings over the past six months and to categorise them into external and internal, regular, *ad hoc* and team meetings.

The analysis revealed that he was spending a staggering 60 hours a month at external meetings and less than three hours a month with his own staff. He set a goal to reduce his outside meetings by twenty hours a month through attending some intermittently and delegating others to his staff. He also set a goal to spend six hours a week with his staff to include monthly "one-on-ones" and a weekly meeting. Now, at the end of each week, he reviews his diary against those two goals and reschedules his time accordingly.

As part of the diary analysis, compare the hours you spent on your major activities in the past six months with the total hours in your week or the amount of time you gave to other activities. And when counting up the hours on meetings or visits, also include the travel and preparation time involved.

Get in Touch with Your Feelings

Apart from analysing a time log or your diary commitments, do not ignore the data on how you feel about the way you are using your time – sometimes the "soft" data is the most compelling for change – your stress level, confusion about your role, the constant day-to-day pressure or just feeling out of control with your time.

One way to get some data on your feelings is to take five minutes each evening to write a brief reflection on the day: What did you achieve? What frustrated your efforts? What will you resolve to do differently tomorrow? If a daily reflection sounds too much then do it weekly, on a Friday, as a part of planning for next week. Alternatively, at times when you feel under pressure take five minutes to get those feelings down on paper as a way of reducing your anxiety and getting more certainty about the cause.

Also involve others in sensing out the soft data by getting their views on how your work style may be frustrating your efforts. As well as getting feedback from your staff on your time style, also get them to reflect on where their own time is going. Managers often end up being overworked and unsupported because they are reluctant to overload their busy staff with even more work – so they do it themselves. But ask yourself this: What are your staff busy doing? If they analysed their time they would find that much of it is taken up with minor routines and urgent tasks that could be reduced or eliminated. Also, remind yourself that it is their job to assist you in achieving your results as a manager and if you are frustrated about the level of assistance you are getting it is most likely because they see their job and priorities differently.

WHAT MANAGERS REALLY DO WITH THEIR TIME

As one of your most critical resources in the job, the only way to get more control of your time is to spend it wisely on the things that contribute most to your effectiveness. The data from over 60 diary and observational studies on how managers use their time reveals a disturbing picture, confirming a view that many businesses today are over-administrated and under-managed.

• Managers Give Very Little Time to their Priorities

Although, by definition, management is about achieving results, managers spend less than 10 per cent of their day on tasks they identify as priorities. Rather than giving concentrated chunks of time to what they see as important, their time tends to be fragmented and unfocused, driven by routine and urgency rather than by challenges or priorities, and they seem to enjoy it that way.

• Few Managers Have a Daily, Weekly or Long-term Plan

While some of the time that managers spend reacting to day-to-day crises is caused by other people, much of it reflects their own lack of planning. Few managers spend even five minutes in the morning planning what they want to get out of the day. Instead they look to their diary for inspiration or busy themselves with the post or e-mail, until the first meeting or interruption sets them on course for the rest of the day.

SOME FACTS

- Less than 10 per cent of the manager's day is spent on priority tasks.

- Managers spend less than 30 per cent of their time on managerial tasks.

- Managers are interrupted on average every 7 minutes.

- 90 per cent of the manager's time is spent on activities of less than 9 minutes.

- 36 – 69 per cent of the manager's time is spent at meetings.

- Thinking time for manager's is less than 5 per cent of their day.

- Senior managers spend less than 3 per cent of their time on strategic issues.

In the longer term, few managers have a monthly plan, medium-term goals or a vision for the future. Yet ask any manager what they need to make more time for, and – surprise, surprise – planning always comes top of the list.

• Managers are Constantly Interrupted

One of the most common excuses for lack of achievement in the job is the volume of interruptions that come at the manager each day. With an average of one interruption every seven minutes from the telephone, drop in visitors or minor crises, managers get the important things done between interruptions.

Although they may only take a few minutes here and there, interruptions account for up to 25 per cent of the manager's day, not only making it difficult for them to give concentrated time to the major tasks in the job but also forcing them to do the most important things at times of the day they have least energy for planning or thinking.

• Managers Make Little Quality Time for their Staff

Although up to 30 per cent of managers' time is spent with staff, most of it is reacting to the immediate problems and issues of the day. Managers give very little time to training their staff, reviewing their performance or counselling and developing them. As a consequence, they often end up doing things themselves that could be done by their staff if they were better informed and more competent.

It is argued by some commentators that in today's environment managers are required to be more flexible to the changing demands of their customers and the competition. An opposing view is that the overwork and stress felt by many managers are symptoms of them not having adapted to an environment which demands that they focus on the important things and let go of the trivia that can so easily fill their day. The solution probably lies somewhere in the balance; that to remain responsive managers have to be flexible to the immediate issues of the day while at the same time being clearly focused on the future. Total flexibility, without plan or direction, is a recipe for chaos and under-achievement, while being inexible and over-scheduled can lead managers to become bureaucratic and unwilling to adapt

What is certain is that managers today are under increasing pressure from a variety of demands on their time. Retaining a healthy balance between what needs to be done for today and what needs to be made happen for the future means developing good habits with your time and minimising the bad habits that can so easily lead to long hours, stress and over-commitment. At the beginning of that journey, more important than solutions is a better understanding of where your time is going and where it needs to go for the future.

ELEPHANTS & ANTS

The biggest obstacle to making better choices with your time is that most people do not know where it is going in the first place. Without a clear sense of where your time is going, it is hard to make choices to do things differently with any certainty that you are going in the right direction.

As a way of reviewing how you are currently using your time, try keeping an occasional time log, review your diary every six months, reflect on your commitments to others and start making more time for yourself to plan for the future.

If you don't know where you are going
You may end up somewhere else

Chapter 3

Keep the End in Mind

Did you hear the story of the airline pilot who announced to the passengers that he had some good news and some bad news. "The good news is we are doing over 600 miles an hour – the bad news is that we're lost." As a manager, you may share similar feelings of being very busy with the wrong things, working hard but not going anywhere.

Not only is overwork and lack of direction a recipe for under-achievement, it is also a common source of stress for managers. In an interview to promote *The Little Book of Calm*, author Paul Wilson identified the two most common sources of job stress as overwork and being out of control with your time. While hard work can be both challenging and energising if it is leading somewhere, without direction or purpose it simply adds to the feeling of being out of control. As Thomas Carlyle once proclaimed "there is nothing more terrifying than activity without insight".

What makes time a complex and difficult resource to manage is that there are competing demands between what has to be done for today and what needs to be done for the future. Although managers are expected to handle the day to day tasks efficiently, they are also expected to achieve results in the longer term; to improve things, to innovate and to develop things. Yet the overwhelming pressure in most organisations today is for managers to be reactive rather than strategic, to be operational rather than managerial. As a consequence the real challenges in managing are absent for many, reflected in a survey by the AMA that identifies more than 78 per cent of managers being dissatisfied with their jobs, and, if they had a choice, would pursue an alternative career – so much for the rewards of managing.

CREATING A CHALLENGE

A career in plastic surgery lead Dr Maxwell Maltz to identify a clear link between self-esteem and challenge in life. In a book called *Psycho-cybernetics*, he recalls how many of the patients who came to his clinic hoped that in some way a change in their physical appearance would change their lives. He found that although surgery worked in a positive way for some patients, for many others it did little to change the way they saw themselves – those who felt good about themselves before surgery continued to feel good afterwards and those who felt they were failures continued to behave as if they still had an ugly face or a physical disability. Concluding that self-esteem comes from what we do in our lives rather than how we see ourselves, he suggests that man is like a bicycle, maintaining his poise and equilibrium only so long as he is going forward towards something.

> *...man is engineered as a goal seeking mechanism, built to conquer the environment, solve problems, achieve goals, and we find no real satisfaction and happiness in life without obstacles to conquer and goals to achieve.*
>
> Dr Maxwell Maltz

The extent to which managers set and meet challenges in the job is also important in defining how they see themselves as managers. While some managers feel overworked and out of control with their time, others, with a clearer sense of what they are trying to achieve, see the same constraints as challenges to succeed. Meeting those challenges not only helps them grow in confidence, it encourages them to set even more ambitious challenges for the future – as Thomas Huxley once wrote: "The rung of a ladder was never meant to rest upon, but only to hold a man's foot long enough to put it somewhere higher."

In summary, the way you act determines how you see yourself and as you see yourself, so you act. The way to become an effective manager is to start behaving like one.

GET A LIFE; GET A VISION

You may have heard the tale of the traveller who came across three artisans cutting stone in a quarry. Out of curiosity he asked them in turn what they were doing. The first who was idling against a wall said, "I am doing what I am told." Another, who was cleaning his implements, said, "I am cutting stone." He moved on to the third who, though busy at work, looked up to inform the traveller, "I am building a cathedral."

While it is sometimes easier to settle for the routine of the job, the benefits of having clear, long-term challenges is that it gives purpose to what you are trying to do as a manager. In addition to providing direction to your own efforts, a clear sense of vision is also important in leading others towards a better future and an antidote to the ever-present activity trap. One way of getting in touch with your aspirations and challenges is by "looking out" at the environment and "looking in" at your values and vision for the future.

Looking Out

Organisations today are much more conscious of the environment than they were ten years ago and many businesses get into trouble because they ignore the competition, new technology and changes in consumer demand. Healthy organisations and effective managers anticipate the changes that are likely for the future and see them as challenges to improve things, to change things and to grow the business.

Take a moment to consider the changing environment in your area for the next year or two. What challenges does it present?

- **Technology**: new or modified products, changing attitudes and uses, user-friendliness, customer expectation.
- **Consumer demand**: for better quality, service, design, ease of use, instant response, cheaper products and services, variety.
- **Competition**: more choice of supplier, cost cutting, new entrants, bigger competitors.
- **Legislation**: social, environmental, medical, working hours, conditions.
- **Labour market**: structure, availability, better qualified, more expectation.
- **Markets**: changes in distribution, demographics, age structure, sophistication.
- **Innovation**: speed, new materials, investment, new systems, processes, markets.

Figure 3.1: External Challenges

Identify three external challenges for your area over the next two to three years. What responses are you currently making to them? What would be a more proactive response for the next year?

	Challenges	Current Response	Better Response
1			
2			
3			

Looking In

Getting direction for the future is also helped by revisiting your personal values and vision. Ask yourself a few basic questions about your role as a manager and where you want to go for the next one to two years.

- What do you want to give more time to or take on as challenges in the job? For example, better teamwork, more openness, greater flexibility, more training.
- Where do you want to be in a year's time that is a better place than now? For example, having a new system in place, new markets for existing products, doubling staff, being the clear market leader.
- Where do you want to go with your values for the next year? For example, develop a customer service programme, get ISO, make changes in work practices or encourage participation.
- Which of these do you identify with as a challenge for the next one to two years?
  1. Increased market share, revenue and productivity.
  2. Better on-time delivery.
  3. Improved customer service, customer retention.
  4. Better teamwork and integration.
  5. Increased team spirit.
  6. Better morale and motivation.
  7. More flexible and empowered staff.

8. Culture of continuous improvement.
9. Achieve a standard, e.g. ISO, quality mark, excellence through people.
10. Reduced waste, downtime, rejects, complaints or overtime.
11. New products and services.
12. Better trained staff.
13. Any others.

Figure 3.2: SWOT Analysis

A systematic way of identifying the challenges in your area is to carry out a SWOT Analysis. Take a sheet of paper and divide it into four boxes. In each of the boxes brainstorm a list of the Internal Strengths (S) and Weaknesses (W), and the External Opportunities (O) and Threats (T). Even better, do the exercise with your team – all it needs is a flip chart and an hour or two.

When you have completed the brainstorm (about ten minutes per box) identify one thing from each box you intend to take on as a challenge for the next year.

S	Quality Products	New Technologies	O
	Good Service	*Changing Demographics*	
	Customer Base	Educated Customers	
Internal			External
W	*Lack of Trained Staff*	Tighter Legislation	T
	Inadequate Systems	*New Competitors*	
	Weak Supervisor	Cheap imports	

Turn Your Aspirations into Goals

While having a clear sense of the challenges and a vision for the future can give you a better sense of where you are going, many of the things that managers want to make happen for the long term are broad and aspirational, such as improving the product range, better teamwork, shorter lead times or increased market share. As such, they are hard to action because they sound like New Year's resolutions – and we all know how long *they* last. It helps in generating commitment to your future aspirations if you make them into SMART goals – Specific, Measurable, Agreed, Realistic and Time bound.

Figure 3.3: Vision into Tasks

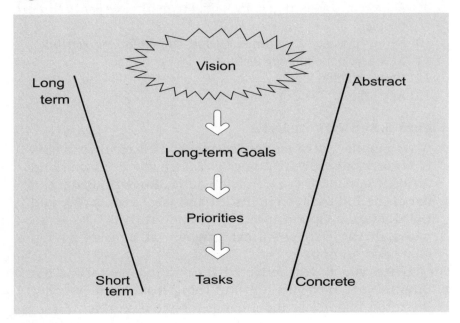

Turning your aspirations into goals is as old as God's command to Noah to: "Build an Ark 30 cubits long and 30 cubits wide in seven months and take on board a male and a female of every animal." In more recent history, when NASA was losing ground to Russian technology, Kennedy gave them new life by articulating the space programme as a goal: "To get a man on the moon and safely back to earth by the end of the decade." Not only do goals provide clear challenges to succeed, they also make the seemingly impossible things possible. For thirteen years the 4-minute mile appeared beyond the reach of athletes until Roger Bannister broke the barrier on 6 May 1954 in a time of 3.59.4 minutes. In the following year over thirteen runners broke the magical 4-minute mile.

Take a little time to identify some goals for the next six to twelve months that will move you in the direction of your vision. Draw up a list of things you could do and select two or three of them for action.

Vision: 3 years • Build team of multi-skilled sales staff to achieve a consistent 80 per cent customer service rating.

Goals: 1 year
- Train all staff in customer service skills.
- Introduce regular two-monthly team meetings.
- Improve the team briefing system.
- Have quarterly job reviews.
- Deal with the three problem people in the department.

Light Many Fires

Although goals can help to make aspirations more concrete, ultimately you keep your aspirations alive by what you do on a daily and a weekly basis. Start the process by having your goals in writing as a constant reminder that you want to achieve things for the future as well as work hard. Involve your staff in creating the goals, or at least share them with your staff, and make sure they are frequently on the agenda of your staff meetings.

Other ways to keep your goals alive include committing dates in your diary when you expect to have them completed, using slogans to capture the spirit of the goal, setting up task groups to manage them, constantly repeating them to others as a way of reminding yourself and finding many ways to walk the talk.

Feargal Quinn built a formidable reputation for the supermarket chain Superquinn through his continuing commitment to customer service. Based on the "boomerang principle", his vision was to provide such a good experience for shoppers that they would return again and again. As part of that process, he does many things to fuel the challenge, through slogans such as: "You came for the prices and stayed for the service", comprehensive staff induction, continuous training, innovations (e.g. bread shops, umbrellas on wet days and assistance for mothers who are shopping for their children). He regularly packs groceries, meets with his suppliers on the floor so they can hear directly from customers and has focus groups where customers are encouraged to complain and contribute to improvements. In a variety of other ways too, such as giving managers tie pins with the letters YCDBSOYA – "you can't do business sitting on your ass" – he reminds his staff that customer service means everyone walking the talk.

Make an appointment with yourself each month to review progress on your long-term goals – diary it as a solid commitment so it happens. Also diary an annual commitment to revisit the environment or your values and vision for the future. Complete a SWOT analysis once a year with your team or involve them in reviewing your values, which inevitably decay unless they are constantly renewed.

> At Intel, managers are rated once a year by their staff on how well they managed the values, such as risk taking, customer orientation and making it a great place to work. Likewise, every McDonald's outlet is audited annually on the management of their core values of quality, cleanliness and service.

Few managers attempt to verbalise their aspirations and goals in the job, almost for fear that expressing them could deny their achievement. However, by not having a clear sense of where you are going you run the risk of succeeding at just one thing – being busy with the ants and ignoring the elephants.

A great deal of energy is available to managers from examining where they want to go and setting out what they want to achieve for the future. Only by having a clear sense of direction can you hope to avoid drifting into short-term efficiency at the expense of longer term effectiveness – remember the saying: "If you don't know where you are going you may end up somewhere else."

ELEPHANTS & ANTS

Managing is not just about doing things for today – it is also about doing things today to improve and develop things for the future. It means creating the same energy for achieving things for the future as you have for doing things for today.

Start getting more direction and energy for the future by making your aspirations and ambitions into clear challenges, sharing them with others and reviewing them frequently to remind yourself that you are there to achieve things as well as get things done. If you do not know where you are going, you may end up somewhere else.

*No matter how efficiently
you do a job*

*If it is the wrong job
it isn't worth doing*

Chapter 4

Focus on the Priorities

While having a vision or clear challenges for the future may help to give you direction as a manager, many people with ambitions and aspirations in life never achieve any of them. How many people who say they have a book to write ever see it published? How many with ambitions to change their careers, get a further qualification, travel the world, get promoted, own their own business or live in another culture ever achieve their ideals? Look back at your early career ambitions. How many have you realised so far?

PROACTIVE AND REACTIVE WORK

The main barrier to turning aspirations into achievements is that managers have two competing demands on their time. On one side is the operational work, which includes routine meetings, paperwork, problem solving and interruptions, and on the other the broader responsibilities, such as meeting targets, achieving deadlines, developing the area and completing projects. Although they may complain about the amount of routine and reaction in their day, managers by and large do not have a problem with that type of work, which usually gets done because it is tangible, short term and familiar – in fact managers enjoy much of it. What managers have much more difficulty finding time for is the proactive side of the job, which is long term and much less demanding of their immediate attention. And in the normal course of events, as Gresham's law states, "routine and urgency tend to drive out the important work".

The essential difference between managing the day-to-day operational work and focusing on the long-term tasks in the job, is that reactive work is largely driven by events and other people, while proactive work has to be made happen. And apart from the practical difficulties of finding time and energy to make the bigger things happen, there is a great deal of organisational pressure on managers to be responsive and short term – often they report to bosses who wants instant reaction and quick results – and what gets rewarded generally gets done.

Figure 4.1: The Reactive/Proactive Balance

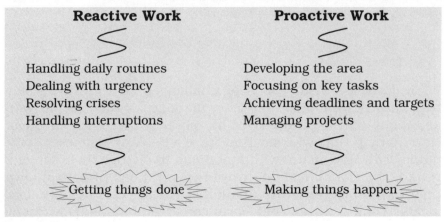

The only way for managers to ensure that they are not overwhelmed by the day-to-day pressures in the job is to have clear challenges and to find ways of getting as energised about the future as they are about the present. There are two important ingredients in becoming proactive as a manager: firstly, knowing what you want to make happen and, secondly, finding the energy to get started and keep going when things get tough.

While getting direction for the future is partly a function of having longer-term aspirations, it also helps to have shorter term priorities to point you in the direction of where you want to go for the next couple of months. But having priorities is not enough; many managers who know where they want to go find it hard to get into their priorities because they lack the *energy* to get started and to keep going, and that comes from making priorities into tasks.

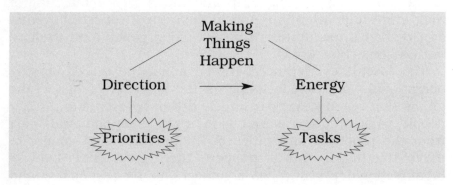

Getting Direction and Focus

Setting priorities in the job is a straightforward exercise. It involves taking five to ten minutes once a month to draw up a list of all the things you would like to achieve or get done in the next few months – it could be two months or six months depending on your preferred time horizon. Apart from considering the things you *have* to get done, also identify the things you *want* to get done. What do you want to achieve or make some headway on in the next couple of months? In five minutes most managers come up with at least ten things they want to get some mileage on in the near future.

However, while it is easy to draw up a wish list, we really only have energy for two or three priorities at any one time. Focus is the key to effectiveness in most walks of life and lack of focus one of the ways in which managers give away their influence and ability to achieve things. The "Golden Rule of Three", which applies to many situations, offers a simple guide in setting priorities, suggesting that more than three is too many – by focusing on too many things you often end up focusing on nothing.

In selecting three priorities for the next couple of months, it is also important to identify the things for which you have real energy. Energy is critical to achieving most challenges in life, whether giving up smoking or passing exams; and energy comes from only two places: anxiety or excitement. Some things we achieve in this life because we are anxious, about our weight or an important deadline, and others because we are excited, about learning a piece of software or a foreign language. As you scan down your wish list, pick three things for which you have real energy now and let the others go, at least for this month. Who knows, next month you may have more energy for other things.

As newly elected president of his tennis club, John was keen to give direction to the members and make some progress in the short term. From a list of challenges for the next year the committee agreed on three as priorities for the next three months.

1) To redecorate the premises.
2) To upgrade the bar food menu.
3) To attract a higher percentage of members on a regular basis.

While not losing sight of the need to run a good tennis programme for the year, having a limited number of priorities for action gave the committee and members a sense of where the club was going, and John a clear brief to succeed as president.

Create Energy for the Priorities

While they may look invitingly simple, trying to make progress on priorities is like trying to eat an elephant: hard to start, difficult to digest and, once started, hard to finish. Yet, it does suggest some practical disciplines for managing priorities.

RULES FOR EATING ELEPHANTS

Rule 1   Make them into a clear challenge.

Rule 2   Break them into bits.

Rule 3   Start wherever the elephant will let you.

Rule 4   Keep your eye on the elephants while you are fighting off the ants.

Many long-term priorities are vague and aspirational, with a familiar ring that suggests they have been around for a while. And, like aspirations to give up smoking or lose weight, the energy for most priorities does not last long.

It helps to energise bigger and more difficult things if you first make them into clear challenges. Rather than committing to "get fit" in the next couple of months set yourself the target of running a 10k mini-marathon in May, losing 10lbs by 30 June or joining a gym and exercising twice a week for the next two months. Making priorities into clear challenges is similar to going for the bullseye rather than aiming at the target – if you miss the bullseye at least you hit the target, while if you aim at the target and miss, you hit nothing.

PRIORITIES

1. To improve Teamwork in my area.

2. To implement a new Distribution System.

CHALLENGES

- Appoint and train three team leaders by 31 March.

- Reach the 24-hour delivery promise to at least 90 per cent of customers by 31 May.

- Organise an offsite day with all staff by 1 June.

- Identify blocks to delivery and set up task group to improve them by 1 January.

Start on the Easy Bits

Although converting priorities into challenges makes them more accessible, they are still difficult to achieve because the energy for most people is in what needs to be done for today rather than what they want to achieve in the next two months. Ask yourself this: when do people get real energy for exams, projects, reports, summer holidays or Christmas? Correct – about a week or ten days before the event or deadline. Things that are two or three months down the road are often left undone until the urgency of a deadline ensures that they are done so stressfully that they won't be taken on as priorities in the future.

The way to make energy for priorities is to look at what you could do in the next week or two to get some quick and easy success (Figure 4.2). If one of your priorities over the next couple of months is to "appoint and train three new team leaders", consider all the short-term tasks you could do in the next week to eat the first piece of the elephant: do up a job description; put an advertisement on the staff notice board; or agree a pay structure with your boss.

Figure 4.2: Break Priorities Into Bits

Take one of your priorities for the next couple of months and brainstorm all the simple things you could do in the next week to get started. Think of simple things, like telephoning someone, having a meeting, reading a book, doing a one page outline or planning a visit. And do not put sequence into the tasks which only kills energy if you find your progress blocked by one step in the sequence.

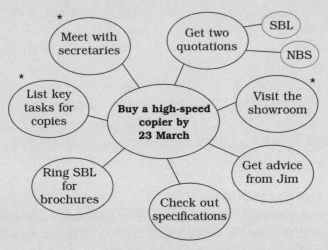

Now, asterisk the three things you will commit to doing immediately, preferably tasks that are accessible because they are cheap, easy or exciting. More important than doing the right things first is doing things that will give you early success.

Not only is it easier to schedule time for short-term tasks than for priorities they also fit the time-frame that is available to managers. Breaking elephants into pieces and starting on the easy bits also guarantees some success in the short term and it is success that breeds energy to go on to the next piece of the elephant.

Keep the Elephants Up Front

In the normal course of events, it is very easy to lose sight of the bigger things to the overwhelming volume of short-term demands on your time. As a way of keeping your longer term priorities in view, have them in writing as visible commitments to action. Also, keep them conspicuous by having them on the wall in front of your desk as a constant reminder that you are there to achieve things as well as do things – with bigger things, "out of sight" generally means "out of mind". At the beginning of each day or week review your long-term priorities to check if there are any tasks you could bring down onto your weekly plan or diary for today or for this week.

Also, keep your priorities in view by getting support from others who could help you achieve them, such as your boss or key staff. Most big challenges in life, like losing weight, writing a book or finishing a thesis, need the support of others to keep you going, or at least not to block your efforts. Keep repeating your priorities to others, as a way of renewing your commitment to them – the best way to give up smoking or lose weight is to keep telling people you are doing it and get them to gently but firmly nag you into action.

Track What you Want to Control

One of the reasons for breaking elephants into bits is it makes them easier to track and control. If one of your priorities is to lose 10 lbs in weight, a few tracking tasks that could help you to get some immediate progress include drawing up a weight loss chart, buying a pair of bathroom scales or weighing yourself today.

And tracking what you are trying to achieve is often enough to make it happen. When a group of new home owners in New Jersey was asked to take part in an experiment on conserving domestic energy, some were given a very challenging target to reduce their electricity consumption by 20 per cent, some an easy target of 2 per cent and others assigned to a control group who were given no target. All three groups were given daily feedback by the researchers updating a graph attached to their patio windows. The results of the experiment showed that those who had a challenging target did best, but equally interesting, those who were just given feedback also significantly reduced their energy consumption.

Simple methods for tracking priorities include setting a target for the number of hours a week you intend to give to a project and recording each hour or half hour as you complete it – many things get done if you simply give them time. Alternatively, if you want to reduce material wastage or improve customer service in your area, agree a standard and share feedback on it each week with your staff – better still, get your staff to record and report the data themselves. If you want to improve one of your personal habits, start recording the number of cigarettes, pieces of chocolate, fruit or hours of sleep you get each day. As a way of tracking progress on projects, set a deadline for completion and break them into mini-deadlines for each stage. If you fail to meet one of the mini-deadlines brainstorm a list of things you could do to get back on track and select three as commitments for next week.

When Jan Carlson took over as President of SAS it was in serious trouble, with losses in excess of $17 million. He soon found that he was heading up a company that had drifted into many things such as charters, holidays and freight and was doing none of them very well. Setting out to re-establish SAS as Europe's premier business airline, he identified punctuality as their number one priority. As a way of monitoring progress, Carlson had a viewing screen installed in his office with details of all flight delays. If there was a problem he would personally ring the airport, sometimes talking directly to the flight crew to resolve the issue or compliment them when they got things right. In one short year SAS became the top on-time airline in Europe.

Review your Progress Frequently

The process of breaking elephants into chunks also makes them easier to manage on a daily basis – it is much easier to schedule simple tasks into your day than to make progress on sometimes vague priorities. Check your priorities frequently and as you get the tasks done acknowledge their completion by ticking them off the list; then identify others as commitments. Also bring new tasks on board as other possibilities come to mind. And when you have completed the initial tasks (Figure 4.3), look for more creative and adventurous tasks to keep your energy for the long haul.

Figure 4.3: Review and Plan

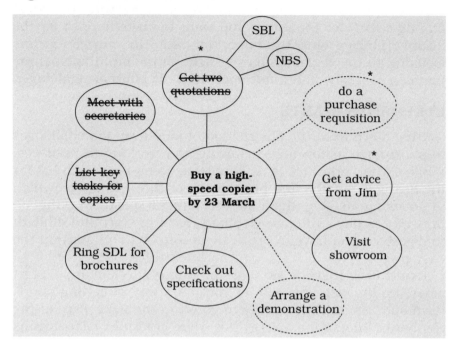

Finally, a simple discipline for ensuring that you renew your priorities on a regular basis is to make a note in your diary on one day each month to draw up a new wish list and select three more priorities. Not only will it give you a sense of moving towards your longer term ambitions but sitting down once a month and doing up a new list will also give you energy for the future. While some priorities may extend over a few months (for example, this book has been a priority for me over the past eight months) others will reach completion and can be replaced with fresh priorities as new challenges become more focal.

Managers are inclined to take priorities for granted, hoping in some way they will get time and energy for the bigger and more strategic things in the job. But while they may be convinced of the need to make things happen as well as do things for today, the evidence is that managers give very little time to what they say is important for the future. Not only are long-term tasks less focal on a day-to-day basis but most of the big things take much longer to complete than was planned because they are often started reluctantly and enthusiasm wanes early on in the process.

The only way to reverse the trap, which sees so many managers overwhelmed by day-to-day operating work, is to start finding energy for the things you want to make happen for the future. Hanging onto the important tasks in your job means focusing on the elephants as you fight off the multitude of ants that can so easily undermine your time and effort as a manager.

ELEPHANTS & ANTS

Getting down from the abstraction of long-term job challenges to short-term action means having and working to priorities. While setting priorities is as simple as doing up a wish list for the next few months and picking two or three things on which to focus, managing them is the difficult part. Working on priorities is like eating an elephant, hard to start and difficult to digest, so you have to break them into bits and start on the easy pieces.

Remember, there is no logic to eating an elephant – start wherever the elephant will let you, as a way of getting short-term success and the energy to go on to the next piece of the elephant. Sustaining energy for your priorities also means finding ways to keep them up front, reviewing them frequently and resetting them monthly.

It isn't the hours you put into the work

It's the work you put into the hours

Chapter 5

Schedule
for the Important Things

In the typical working day many things get done because they are part of the familiar routine, e.g. opening the post, checking e-mails or responding to post-it notes. Not only do they offer managers the opportunity of an easy reward but they are also part of the buzz in the job. Other things to which managers also have little difficulty committing their time include institutionalised activities, like meetings, visits or appointments, which are easily scheduled into their day and are seldom questioned.

Apart from the routine or institutionalised activities, some tasks are easy to do because they are attractive opportunities even when managers are weighed down with work and over-commitment. Imagine your boss telling you that he wanted someone to represent the company on a ten-day all-expenses paid fact-finding visit to Thailand. While recognising that you are the obvious person to go, he is also aware of your work pressure and suggests that you take an hour or two think about whether you could make the time. Well, do you think you can find ten days? Probably, if you are like other managers who have been posed the same question. How do you do it? Easy. You take your diary and a pen, draw a line through the ten days and over the top write one word: Thailand.

> *Ask any manager for his major continuing problem and he will normally reply "time". Time to think, time to plan, time to talk with my people. Yet the same man finds the time for food and for sleep, for Sundays and for holidays. But these are institutionalised priorities – time for the future is not.*
>
> *Understanding Organisations*
> Charles Handy

But, unlike institutionalised activities or the attractive overseas conference, managers find it much more difficult to get time for their longer term challenges, such as developing teamwork, improving communications or completing projects. Those kind of things do not get done unless they are scheduled into the manager's day, week or month.

TIME FOR IMPORTANCE

Managing time is all about making choices, many of which are dictated by urgency, which often drives out the important things, especially where tasks are not urgent.

> I met a client for lunch the other day. He had arranged the meeting to discuss management development needs in his area. As we sat down to lunch his mobile phone rang and, from the conversation, I gathered it was a minor issue. As telephone reception was poor in the dining room he excused himself to continue his conversation in the lobby and after a few minutes I decided to go ahead and start my meal. Twenty-five minutes later, when he returned, I had finished my lunch, his was cold, and very soon after he had to excuse himself to get to another appointment. We never did get to discuss the issue of developing his people. Interestingly enough, a couple of weeks earlier his boss had described him as an "operational manager".

Both the urgent and the important things have to be managed into the day – the trick is not letting urgency become the only driving force in the job. As well as making appropriate responses to the routine demands you also need to get mileage out of your day by finding time for the longer term issues. Scheduling your time effectively means pushing the barriers of importance so that you end up doing the things that have to be done, but also making time to achieve the things you want to get done.

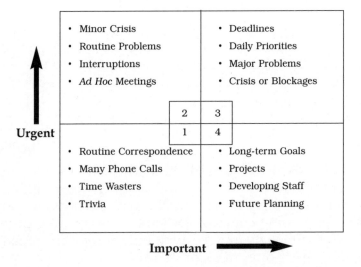

Box 1: Unimportant and Non-urgent Tasks

As a manager, you should be trying to reduce the amount of time you give to some things, either by not doing them at all or giving them less time. Less urgent or routine things, such as paperwork or handling queries, could be given to others – why not let someone else open the post or attend that routine meeting? Also, consider doing the less important things at times of the day when you have least energy or less time – open your post, check your e-mails or chase people up in the afternoons.

Box 2: Urgent but Unimportant Tasks

Urgent but less important things, such as minor crises or routine problems, could be dealt with by giving them sparing amounts of time immediately or scheduling them for later in the day. Many of the routinely urgent issues could also be handled by developing procedures or training others to deal with them.

Box 3: Urgent and Important Tasks

Some things are urgent and important because there is a deadline to meet or because priorities shift, e.g. a key customer needs material urgently to complete a rush order, or a machine has gone down and decisions have to be made to get it back into production. In that event, the daily schedule may have to be rearranged to respond immediately to that task or to do the most urgent piece now and deal with the rest later.

Box 4: Important but Non-urgent Tasks

Other things are important but are not urgent. Many of the functions that are critical to management effectiveness, such as planning, reviewing progress on projects, developing new systems, or improving quality and service, are not driven by routine or urgency but by managers giving them solid chunks of time. Proactive work that has no immediate urgency is in danger of being deferred unless it is diarised or identified as a priority and broken into chunks that can be managed on a daily or a weekly basis.

While the tasks in boxes 1 and 2 need to be organised effectively into your day, tasks in boxes 3 and 4 need to be scheduled to make them happen. Simple ways of scheduling time for the important things in your day, week and month include the use of a "to do" list, a weekly planner or a diary.

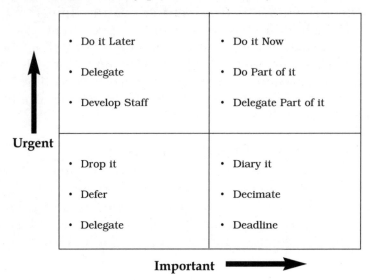

CARPE DIEM: SEIZE THE DAY

One of the most common habits at work is keeping lists of things we are trying to get done in the day. The main problem with lists, apart from the fact that they tend to get longer and longer, is that most people start on the easy things first, the logic being, "I'll get rid of the easy things and then I'll get into the bigger ones". Of course it does not work that way – usually we find more and more easy things to prevent us from getting into the important things, which are relegated to the back end of the afternoon or transferred to yet another list for tomorrow.

> *My mother was an inveterate list maker throughout her 90 years. We grew to dread helping her when we came back to stay at the farm, as her list contained such items as: paint barn, fence farm, plant lower field, bring in harvest. One morning as I sat watching her finish her daily list, she smiled with satisfaction and crossed off the first item. "Mother," I said, "how could you have already accomplished something?" Then I looked over her shoulder. She had crossed out the first two words: "Make list".*

Opel Nestingen

One simple way to ensure that you balance urgency and importance in your day is to keep a "to do" list. While it starts life as a simple list, what makes a "to do" list into a management tool is that you prioritise the activities as *A*s, *B*s, *C*s and *D*s, and work to those priorities (Figure 5.1). The *A*s are tasks that you must get done today and there should never be more than three. The *B*s are things you should get done today – the *A*s-in-waiting that may become priorities but only when you get the *A*s done. The *C*s are things you want to put on the list so you do not forget them and *D*s are things you want to give to others to do.

> One of the most quoted stories on time management concerns Charles Schwab, former President of Bethlehem Steel and his efficiency expert Ivy Lee. When Schwab asked for some advice on how to speed up his work flow, Lee promised that in 20 minutes he could improve his efficiency by 50 per cent. Handing him a piece of paper he told him to write down his six most important tasks for tomorrow and to number them in order of importance. He suggested that Schwab start on item 1 first thing in the morning and work on it until it was finished and then go onto item 2, and not to be too concerned about how many things he completed in the day, since he would always be working on the most important things first. He advised Schwab to persist until he was convinced of its usefulness and to have his men try it too and send him a cheque for what he thought the idea was worth. A few weeks later Lee received a cheque for $25,000 as payment for the most profitable lesson Schwab had ever learned as a manager.

The secret of working with a "to do" list is to start as early as possible on the three *A*s, for two reasons. The first is that most people have their peak energy early in the day, somewhere between 8.00 am and 11.00 am, so hitting the *A*s early means you are working on the most important things at times of the day when you have your best mental energy. Conversely it also means you are working on the less important things at times of the day when you have least mental energy.

A second reason for starting early on the *A*s is that getting an early success on one of your important tasks is the best way of creating energy for the rest of the day. When you have completed the three *A*s, simply reprioritise some of the *B*s into *A*s – in that way you are always doing the first things first.

Using a To "Do List"

- Review or redo your "to do" list first thing in the morning.

- Check your long-term priorities and bring tasks down onto the list.

- Prioritise the tasks as *A*s, *B*s, *C*s and *D*s.

- Start early on the *A*s.

- Re-prioritise the activities as you go through the day.

- Keep the list on your desk as a reminder to do the first things first.

TIPS ON KEEPING A TO DO LIST

Keep the main thing the main thing at all times. One of the most common frustrations shared by managers is of not getting sufficient mileage out of their efforts in the day. It helps if you get a "good" start on the day by deciding where you want to go with it and focusing your attention on the important things first. Get the pleasure of crossing the *A*s off the list as you complete them, and at the end of the day it is easy to see whether it was a productive or a busy day: Did you get the *A*s done or was it mainly *C*s and *B*s you completed? While starting on the *A*s is no guarantee that you will get everything done in the day, tackling them first means that you are always focusing on the most important things.

Eat the elephants in chunks. As you do up your "to do" list each morning make sure that it reflects what you want to get done for the long term as well as for today. If you have broken your major priorities into tasks, see if you can draw any of them down onto your "to do" list for today. If some tasks are too big to do as daily tasks then break them into even smaller pieces that can be done in a half hour or an hour in the day.

Figure 5.1: To Do List

TO DO LIST	
B	Invoice Kintech
A	Write IDB proposal
C	Check progress on CS
B	Book flight – London
A	Ring Frank Magee
D	Chase up DCL notes
C	Arrange meeting Tim Lyons

Use the golden rule of three. One of the big temptations with "to do" lists is making more than three things into As on the basis that everything is important. But the problem with having five or six things as As is that you are rapidly getting back to a simple list again and you still have to make a choice about which tasks to do first. Discipline yourself to having no more than three As on your list at any one time and even if you complete them early, simply re-prioritise some of the Bs into As. Tasks which are Bs this morning may well become As this afternoon and items which are Cs today may well become As tomorrow.

Plan the work and work the plan. While a "to do" list gives you a sense of where you want to go with today, it is not a timetable for the day – the beauty is that it gives you both focus and flexibility. Should something urgent or important arise during the day you may have to add it to your list as an A, and if during the day there is a minor crisis to distract you from what you are trying to get done, you may have to forget the list for a while, but always with the intention of getting back to it as soon as possible. The fact that you cannot plan everything does not mean you should not plan.

THANK HEAVEN FOR MONDAYS

It is all too easy to get to Friday with the uncomfortable feeling that it was a hell off a week but you have little to show for all your efforts. Like the cowboy who jumped onto his horse and rode off in all directions, the danger is giving away your energy by trying to go in too many directions at once. One way of avoiding the dangerous drift into "busyness" is to get a clear sense of direction at the beginning of the week, to monitor your progress as you go through the five days and, on Friday, to review your success as a way of planning for the next week.

Allow yourself five minutes on Monday morning to plan what you want to get done with your week. List all the jobs you need to get done in the next five days and select three of them as priorities (Figure 5.2). Break them into smaller tasks, such as writing something, telephoning someone, reading something or meeting someone, and prioritise each task, with no more than three as As. Start into the As on Monday and as you go through the week reprioritise the list, making the Bs and Cs into As. At the end of the week review what kind of week it was: was it efficient in the sense that you got the routine things done or were you effective in getting the important things completed?

Figure 5.2: Weekly Planner

Priorities	Tasks	A/B/C/D
1. *Arrange Pascale visit*	Memo to Gerry	C
	Book hotel	A
	Get flight details	C
	Check bookings	D
*		
2. *Finish appraisal reports by Wednesday*	Arrange to meet Dan	A
	Complete forms	A
	Set date on review meeting	B
	File copies	D
*		
3. *Make decision on purchasing copier*	Check brochures	C
	Ring 3 companies	D
	Get quotes – 2 suppliers	D

TIPS FOR MANAGING A WEEKLY PLANNER

Combine your weekly and daily plans. The place to have a weekly planner is on the wall in front of your desk as a reminder of the weekly challenges and your progress on them. As you complete each task cross it off the list and re-prioritise the rest. Alternatively, you could draw tasks down from your weekly planner onto a "to do" list and prioritise them as daily activities.

As MD of a computer services company, Detta has a one-hour meeting with her management team every Monday morning from 9.00–10.00 am. In that hour they each report what was achieved in the previous week and how it relates to their long-term priorities. They also use the time to share their priorities for this week. At that meeting, they have an opportunity to ask their colleagues for support in advance of looking for assistance – as a result there are no surprises and most important issues can be left until the next Monday meeting.

Share your weekly challenges with others. As a way of reminding your staff what you are trying to get done with your week share your priorities with them. If there are tasks on your weekly planner that you want to delegate to others, do it early in the week, and put a reminder in your diary to monitor progress on them sometime in the middle of the week – do not leave checking on whether things have been done until Friday.

MAKE APPOINTMENTS TO YOURSELF

Most people use a diary as an *aide memoir*, in case they forget dates or their commitments to others. Managers also get some comfort from having a full diary, which conveniently lets them off the hook with having to plan their day or week – all they have to do is follow the diary. The main problem is that many of the things we commit to our diaries should probably not have been agreed at all, and many things consigned to diaries, such as meetings and appointments, are for the benefit of others rather than commitments to our own priorities.

Using a Diary

- At the beginning of each week block out time in your diary for tasks such as planning or project work.

- Review the monthly priorities frequently and schedule time for them in your diary.

- Record deadlines on delegated tasks and monitoring dates along the way.

- Record trigger dates to remind you to review and reset your monthly priorities.

One way to start making more effective use of your diary is to block out chunks of time for the things you want to get done and not to let anything get in the way of these commitments (Figure 5.3). Also, build some breathing space into potentially time-consuming commitments to others by promising to come back in a day or two to confirm a meeting or an appointment. Stop taking your diary into meetings if you tend to make commitments that you later regret, and always ask yourself if there is an easier way of doing things that would take less time (such as exchanging a couple of e-mails or having a phone conversation).

Figure 5.3: Diary

10 **Monday** (11) November	11 **Tuesday** (11) November	12 **Wednesday** (11) November	13 **Thursday** (11) November	14 **Friday** (11) November	15 **Saturday** (11) November
Priorities	*Priorities* Letter UK Plan TCT	*Priorities* Finish IRT report	*Priorities* Plan Deco CBU	*Priorities* Plan job reviews	*Priorities*
8...............	8...............	8...............	8...............	8...............	8...............
30	30 Plan TCT	30	30	30 LPTs	30
9...............	9...............	9...............	9...............	9...............	9...............
30	30	30	30 Plan Deco	30	30
10...............	10...............	10...............	10...............	10...............	10...............
30	30 Letter UK	30	30	30	30
11...............	11...............	11...............	11...............	11...............	11...............
30	30	30 IRT Report	30	30	30
12...............	12...............	12...............	12...............	12...............	12...............
30	30	30	30	30	30
1...............	1...............	1...............	1...............	1...............	1...............
30	30	30	30	30	30
2...............	2...............	2...............	2...............	2...............	2...............
30	30 Review JD Project	30	30	30	30
3...............	3...............	3...............	3...............	3...............	3...............
30	30	30 IRT Report	30 MBWA	30 Job Review	30
4...............	4...............	4...............	4...............	4...............	4...............
30	30	30	30 Check DF Letter	30	30
5...............	5...............	5...............	5...............	5...............	5...............

TIPS ON USING A DIARY

Make time to think. Start using your diary to block out time for thinking or long-term planning, neither of which need to be solitary reflections. Schedule an hour this week to scan a few journal articles, to write up an outline plan for the next three months or to have a free-wheeling meeting with a couple of colleagues on a marketing campaign or a new product development.

Most people think only once or twice a year. I have made an international reputation for myself by thinking once or twice a week.

George Bernard Shaw

Chunk your diary commitments. The weekly planner or "to do" list can be combined with a diary by blocking out specific hours in the day or week to get certain tasks done, such as finishing a report, drafting a letter or planning a presentation. Alternatively, plan to spend one hour this Tuesday morning on a project as a way of getting some initial success on what might otherwise be an overwhelming job. Committing an hour to planning a difficult assignment is often enough to see it a bit more clearly and manageable.

If a big task is likely to take four or five hours to complete make it easier for yourself by breaking it into hourly chunks and scheduling an hour on five separate days. Most authors break the long and solitary task of writing a book into chunks by committing themselves to a couple of hours writing each day or to writing a certain number of words a day. I personally use a stopwatch to work an hour at a time on my bigger tasks and, at the end of an hour, reward myself with a 15-minute break.

Schedule important tasks into the mornings. One of the most interesting pieces of data emerging from time log analyses is how many routine activities are scheduled into the mornings. As much as possible, schedule your most important tasks into the mornings and the less demanding things into the afternoons when you have least mental energy. Most routine meetings are better held in the afternoons, as is routine correspondence, managing by wandering around, responding to telephone messages or answering queries.

People who say they are too busy to exercise are often too busy to worry about their kids – sometimes they are too busy for anything. I tell them, if the President of the United States of America can make time, they can.

President Bush, a regular jogger.

Block out time to yourself. One of the major stress factors today is the feeling that other people and events are controlling your time. Yet many managers who complain about feeling out of control with time also let others decide their appointments or determine the length of their meetings and telephone calls. In an effort to reclaim his time, Robert Townsend, then President of Avis, decided to sack his secretary and to answer his own phone. He claimed that it allowed him to decide when to call people back or whether he was available for interruptions – at all other times he instructed the receptionist to take full messages and let people know when he would reply. It may sound unrealistic but if you need more time for planning and thinking, or simply for doing the things you want to get done with your day, then make sure you do not leave yourself totally at the mercy of others.

Plan to relax. As a way of avoiding the sort of over-commitment that leads to stress, schedule some time in your diary for exercise or relaxation before you start making commitments to others. Decide early in the year when you are going to take your holidays and schedule a few short breaks into the year as solid commitments to yourself. Schedule personal time for exercise, for your family or for networking and where possible make them regular commitments so they become a routine part of your weekly or monthly schedule (e.g. every Thursday evening for the gym or a family event on the first Monday of every month).

> *Over the years I've had many executives come to me and say with pride, "Boy, last year I worked so hard that I didn't take any vacation." It's actually nothing to be proud of. I always feel like responding, "You dummy. You mean to tell me that you can take responsibility for an $80 million project and you can't plan two weeks out of the year to go off with your family and have some fun?"*

> Lee Iaccocca

As a manager, it is all too easy to end up being over-involved with daily routines that could be dealt with by others or spending most of your time fighting fires. Apart from making time for the operational parts of the job, you also need to make time for the things you really want to get done by scheduling time for them. And scheduling time for the real challenges in the job is also the best way of ensuring that you give less time to the things you should be letting go to others.

ELEPHANTS & ANTS

Apart from getting more focus on the things you want to achieve for the future you also have to make time for the important things otherwise they will inevitably get side tracked by urgency and routine. And most important things in this life do get done if you give them time, like passing exams, getting fit or completing a project. Rather than looking for better ways to organise your busyness, start to use devices like the To Do List, Weekly Planner or your Diary to schedule time for the things you want to make happen. Also schedule the important things into your peak energy time, which for most people is the mornings. Reverse the habit of using your best hours in the day for the routine things and trying to get into the important things at times of the day when you have least energy.

*Delegation means letting go of
what you want to hang on to*

*And hanging on to
what you want to let go*

Chapter 6

Delegate the Routine and Urgency

Why is it that so many managers are driven by routine and urgency rather than by the important tasks in their job? Why is it that many managers see themselves as responsible for everything and so many of their staff see themselves responsible for nothing? Why are so many managers stretched and overworked while their staff feel under-utilised and bored? Why do so many managers end up doing what they should patently be getting other people to do?

One of the main excuses used by managers for doing things they should be giving to others is that it is easier to do it themselves. However, the problem with doing things yourself is that others never learn to do them, and over time come to regard them as part of your job. Lack of trained staff is another excuse offered by managers for doing the work of others: "I can't give it to Jack, he is really busy." Managers rarely challenge how busy their staff are – most people end up being busy, but busy doing what?

However, the most common reason for managers continuing to hang on to what they should be giving away to others has little to do with staff. Managers continue to hang on to much of the routine in the job because it is familiar territory and the human condition is that we do not let go of familiar things easily. How many of you have still got cupboards or attics full of old schoolbooks, clothes or letters you should have got rid of years ago? How many people stay in dead-end jobs or hang on to bad relationships because it is difficult to let go?

You spent your life sitting on brambles and wouldn't get up in case someone took your place.

Hugh Leonard

Letting go of familiar and comfortable routines is essentially a function of having other things on which to focus. One example is the Olympic athletes who, in the lead up to the Olympic Games, give up many things, including their eating habits, their social lives, their savings and even their jobs. They have little difficulty letting go because they have their sights clearly set on qualifying for the Games, improving on their personal best, representing their country or winning a medal. Likewise, in the absence of clear goals and priorities, it is difficult for managers to let go of the comfort of daily routine and urgency, much of which in theory is the work of their staff.

But apart from finding it easier to delegate if you have clear challenges in your own job, it also helps if you treat delegation as a broad process for letting go rather than simply about giving more work to your staff. There are in fact four ways to let go of things that take up time in your job.

1. By giving more responsibility to your staff.
2. By saying "no" more often to those who dump on you from above without appreciating your priorities.
3. By pushing things back to colleagues who may have found you a convenient place to dump their problems.
4. By using the waste paper basket as a tool in delegation. The "law of calculated neglect" reminds us that many things if left alone will simply go away.

Figure 6.1: Letting Go

Draw up a list of the things you would like to let go of in your job. For each activity estimate the amount of time you currently spend and the amount by which you would like to reduce that commitment. Use the four strategies in delegation as a guide to identifying how many hours you could let go each week. Pick one as a priority for the next month and find ways to track your success.

Task	Current Hours	Proposed Hours	Saving	Methods
Routine Meetings	8	5	3	• Delegate attending the monthly meeting to Jim • Reduce own meetings by 1/2 hour
Travelling	12	6	6	• Meet managers half way • Take the train

LETTING GO OF REAL RESPONSIBILITY

While managers generally recognise the need to say "no" more often to others or to push back problems to their colleagues, one of the main obstacles to letting go is the difficulty of getting staff to share their responsibilities in the job. Many of the important things you are trying to get done as a manager require the commitment of your staff, not just a willing pair of hands. If, for example, you ask one of your staff to photocopy some notes for an upcoming conference, at best you are delegating work because the task is clear and unambiguous, you can see them doing it and can check the results. If, on the other hand, you ask them to take complete responsibility for the administrative workload at the conference, you are letting go of a much broader task where the person has discretion in how they do it and you cannot control their input so easily. The essential difference between delegating work and responsibility is that letting go of responsibility also means you have to trust people.

Did you hear the story of the climber who fell off a cliff face and managed to save himself by grabbing a small shrub growing from the rock. Suspended in mid air, he yells out, "Is there anybody up there."

After a couple of seconds a voice booms back, "Yes, I am here."

"Who is it?" shouts the climber.

"It is God," booms back the voice,"I will save you."

"What shall I do?" asks the climber.

Back comes the voice, "Let go of the branch and I will catch you."

A minute goes by before the anxious voice starts up again, "Is there anyone else up there?"

Letting go to others does not mean blind trust, if things go wrong it is still your responsibility. Yet managers do have to learn to trust their staff with real responsibility and the only way to do that is by giving them time. Although, as a manager, you may believe that you already spend enough time with your staff, most of those daily contacts are on routine issues or problems. Getting to the point where you can trust your staff with almost the same degree of responsibility as yourself requires "quality time", to clarify what you want from them, to get them to take ownership for tasks and to encourage and recognise them for sharing responsibility. As with personal relationships, you do not learn to trust people unless you spend time developing and sustaining the relationship in four important ways.

1. Tell your Staff What you Want

Over 70 per cent of employees in a recent survey admitted that they were unclear about what their boss wanted from them or how their job performance would be measured. Not only are managers unclear about what they want from their staff but they also have a habit of expressing their demands in vague language, such as "I want you to 'deal with'... 'handle'... 'liaise'... or 'co-ordinate'". Managers also give mixed messages to their staff, such as "I want you to take full responsibility, but let me know if there are problems" or "Do it your way but get my input." And when asked if they are clear about what they are being asked to do, most staff give the non-committal response, "Yes, I think so."

Apart from being unclear about what they want from their staff, managers also believe that saying things once is enough. Even young children learn that if you want something you have to ask for it more than once – the first time you ask for an ice cream or a bar of chocolate you have not even been heard. Similarly, it is not enough to tell your staff once what you want from them, you have to find a variety of ways of reminding them so they hear the message clearly above the other demands in the job.

One of the best ways to remind your staff of their responsibilities is to agree goals with them (Figure 6.2). A simple process involves sitting down individually or as a group and talking about the challenges in their job for the next two to three months. Out of that discussion get them to identify two or three things as priorities and identify tasks that could help them eat the first part of the elephant over the next week or two. Keep a copy of their goals and encourage progress by asking periodically how they are doing. At the end of each month have a short review meeting as a way of rewarding their progress and coach them on finding additional tasks to fuel the next part of the journey.

Figure 6.2: Agree Goals with your Staff

John agreed two goals with Mary at her three-monthly review. As a way of relieving him of some of the administrative work in the training department, he wanted her to take on the purchasing of all training course materials, while Mary identified a need to develop her skills at computer graphics. Agreeing both of them as goals, John helped Mary to identify tasks for the next month that would help her make some progress in both areas.

Goals – 3 months	Tasks – 1 month
Take on ordering of all supplies by 30 June	Meet with two suppliers
	Draw up stock sheet
	Price articles in stock
	Get catalogue from suppliers
Get basic certificate in computer graphics by 28 August	Install software on PC
	Book three lessons
	Two hours a week coaching
	Check requirements for certificate

As the month went by, Mary tackled tasks that she could schedule into her week and John was able to give her encouragement and reward as he saw her making progress. At the end of the month, they sat down for fifteen minutes to review the task list and talk about what she intended to do in the next month.

2. Get Ownership and Commitment

One of the most frustrating aspects of giving responsibility to others is the feeling that they are not fully committed to the task. Real ownership for delegation is different than head nodding – ownership is something that is taken and cannot be assumed. Ownership is also rejected by staff in many subtle ways when they feel they are being dumped on, or find their boss taking back responsibility by interfering in the detail.

As a manager, you need to make time to coach your staff so they take ownership, but you also need to resist the temptation to tell them how to do it, otherwise the task still remains your responsibility – if things go wrong it was your way. On the other hand giving broad responsibility to someone without supporting them is dumping and when people feel dumped on they have many ways of getting back at you.

> Jim decided to involve his staff in planning a major sales conference. As a group they had several planning meetings and everyone knew their individual responsibilities for the three days. But on the first day of the conference, Jim's style changed. Instead of leaving his staff to do their tasks, he began to interfere in the smallest detail, pulling them up on minor issues, grabbing things back from people if there was the slightest problem and harassing them to do things the way he wanted them done. By the end of the first day, his staff were beginning to lose their motivation and confidence and Jim was becoming increasingly involved in the detail, as he saw lack of responsibility in his staff.

Coaching is a process for helping people commit to a task and getting them energised about the journey. Professional coaches rarely tell their charges what to do, instead they inspire them, using two basic skills. Firstly, they "listen", to get them talking and to encourage them to think things through for themselves: "Where do you see the project in three months' time?" "How would you tackle the problem?" "What are your options on this?" "Where would you like to start?" "What's a first step?". Secondly, coaches use "feedback" – providing positive encouragement or correction by giving their picture, e.g. "I feel really good about your progress", "Your sales are 20 per cent above target", "I had three more complaints about service in your area last week".

In a study carried out on communications in a public utility, 76 per cent of the foremen reported always getting ideas from their staff on job issues; however, only 16 per cent of subordinates reported being so consulted by their bosses.

Tell your people what you want and coach them on how to do it. Get the pleasure of seeing them take control and being available if they need help.

3. Monitor What you Give Away

You never completely let go of responsibility, you share it – if something goes wrong, it is still your neck on the line. For your sake, and for the benefit of your staff, you need to follow up what you give away but you also need to make sure that you do not undermine your staff's confidence. There are a number of unobtrusive ways to monitor delegation.

• **MBWA (managing by wandering around)**: commit regular chunks of time in your diary or "to do" list to make casual contacts with your staff to find out how things are going.

• **Naive listening**: rather than asking about the detail of a task, use open-ended questions, such as "Where are you at?", "How is it going?", "What obstacles are you meeting?"

• **Group reviews**: get your team to review progress on their goals in public where they can get affirmation and feedback from the group. In that way they are being challenged by their peers rather than by the boss.

• **Regular one-on-ones**: have frequent "off-the-job" chats with your staff and schedule time for them. At those meetings, which need only to be ten or fifteen minutes a month, keep the balance between listening and talking to about 70 per cent to 30 per cent. Give your staff a real chance to hear themselves and always have something in store to reward them.

• **Delegation checklist**: how often have you given a job to one of your staff only to forget who you gave it to, how long ago or when the person agreed to have it completed? A simple and effective way of keeping track of what you give to others is to keep a delegation checklist (Figure 6.3).

As you identify tasks in your job you want to delegate just add them to the list. When you allocate them to one of your staff, note the initials of that person and the date you allocated the task. Also agree a due date if the task does not have to be done immediately or has to be completed for a critical date. And preferably let the person commit to a date for completion or alternatively let them know that a task has to be done for a particular meeting or deadline. Commit the due dates to your diary together with one or two dates on which you will monitor progress.

Keep the delegation checklist somewhere visible, possibly on the wall in front of your desk, so that you have a clear and continuing sense of what your staff have completed and what is still in the pipeline. You might also consider making the list public so that others can see what their colleagues are doing. Not only is the delegation checklist a simple tool for retaining some sense of control on the tasks you give away to others – it works.

Figure 6.3: Delegation Checklist

N	A		DD
BC	20/8	Type up Climate Survey	30/9
CA	20/8	Get 4 Copies – Workbook	
CA	22/8	Regional Meetings/Agenda	
CA	22/08	Chase up GRT Proposal	
AV	1/9	Make Labels for Files	
FM	1/9	Make Changes in MT Book	21/10
CA	1/9	Get Proofs from Claire	
LT	1/9	Prepare Notes for Jones Meeting	
AV	20/9	Do Acetates on VT Presentation	30/10

4. Reward and Recognise Progress

Like most challenges in life, people take on greater levels of responsibility for the recognition of others. Although your staff may not volunteer to take on extra work, even for more money, they will often do things for someone they respect.

In psychology, the simple *law of effect* says a lot about motivation in stating that "things which are rewarded tend to be repeated and things which are unrewarded tend to be extinguished". In encouraging children to take responsibility for their learning, parents have no problem using a great deal of recognition and praise to encourage their efforts. While the effect of praise and encouragement on children is clear, most managers still undervalue the power of recognition on their staff, finding it much easier to criticise them for what they fail to achieve than praise them for what they get right.

While some managers intuitively know how to get the best out of their people, for most it means scheduling time to reward and recognise the behaviours you want to encourage. And apart from recognising the good performers, who often know they are doing well, it is also important to find ways to encourage the poor performers by praising them for what they are doing approximately right rather than waiting for them to do things exactly right.

Identify two things from the following list that you could do to improve reward and recognition in your area (do not plan to do more than two things otherwise it may appear that you have read a book). Schedule those activities into your diary as solid commitments and make time for them in the next month.

- Start having monthly one-on-ones.
- Celebrate project completion or meeting targets.
- Spend more time with poor performers.
- Have occasional off-site meetings to share views.
- Have an ideas or suggestion scheme.
- Draw up a training plan.
- Celebrate birthdays or anniversaries.
- Do more MBWA.
- Regularise team briefings to tell your staff how things are going.
- Have team meetings at which staff report progress on their goals.
- Reward one piece of good work a day.
- Send thank you notes for jobs well done.
- Set up task groups and get staff to chair them.
- Give one piece of encouragement each day.
- Get more personal details of staff – children, hobbies, commitments, etc.

EMPOWER YOUR STAFF TO EXCEL

The control function that was traditionally exercised by middle managers, has given way in most organisations to more participative and hands-off approaches aimed at encouraging staff to share responsibility for broader issues, such as quality, service and innovation. Developing a participative culture that pushes responsibility down to lower levels also means that managers have to adopt styles of supervision that empower their staff to see beyond the narrow confines of a job description. Empowerment means identifying the future challenges in the area and inviting your staff to share those challenges by raising their expectations of themselves.

Teachers and leaders share a state secret – that when they expect high performance of their charges they increase the likelihood of high performance.

John Gardner

While it is commonly accepted that good coaches inspire athletes to produce peak performances and parents often motivate children to excel beyond their years, the implication is that managers must do the same if they are to get their staff on board with the real organisational challenges for the future. Some of the ways in which managers can raise individual and group expectations are by communicating an exciting vision for the future, setting clear standards and getting their staff to set challenging rather than incremental goals.

In addition, studies clearly show that successful people in all walks of life are empowered not so much through an incremental process of improvement but by taking on demanding and sometimes risky job challenges which develop their confidence in dealing with instability and change. Some of the most common experiences reported by successful middle managers include:

- being thrown in at the deep end;
- having to clear up a mess;
- being assigned a major challenge;
- taking a career risk;

- having to get results to a tight deadline;
- having to make presentations to senior managers.

PUSH BACK THE MONKEYS

One of the major time traps for managers is the volume of problems that come at them from below. Contrary to the view that delegation is a top-down process, most delegation is in fact upwards: of problems, crises and interruption. Not only do managers waste a great deal of their time responding to "monkeys" from staff but their staff learn little from the process except that the next time they have a problem to refer it straight to the manager.

Keeping "monkeys" with subordinates is critical to preventing the levels of reverse delegation that see managers spending a great deal of their time on minor issues and their staff learning very little about taking on extra responsibility.

Rules for Keeping "Monkeys" at Bay

- Encourage your staff to come up with solutions rather than problems.

- Resist giving advice – instead ask questions (e.g. "What do you suggest?" or "What are the options?").

- Have daily or weekly staff meetings at which issues can be raised and dealt with by the group.

- Have a time in the day when you are not willing to be interrupted by staff.

- Agree procedures for dealing with recurring problems.

- Make time to train your staff and only be available for support after that.

- Reward your staff for solving their own problems.

While most managers complain about overwork and pressure in the job, many staff complain about how little their abilities and potential are used by their managers. In a study of first-line managers 25 per cent reported using only a third of their abilities and over half said they were using between 30 and 60 per cent of their skills.

If the well-worn epithet "people are our greatest asset" is to become a reality then managers have to find ways to translate the time they spend doing things themselves into "quality time", aimed at developing the confidence and abilities of their staff. Only by letting go of the urgent and routine tasks and sharing real responsibility with others can managers hope to get the time they need to address the uncertain and critical challenges in their own jobs.

ELEPHANTS & ANTS

Managing is by definition about getting results through other people. And it is difficult to get the space and energy you need for the major results in your own job unless you also learn to let go of responsibility to others. Paradoxically, letting go means making more time for your staff, to clarify what you want from them, to get them to take ownership, to monitor what you give away and to reward them for sharing your responsibilities. With the best will in the world unless you schedule quality time for training and coaching, for one-on-one chats, for goal setting and MBWA, they will not happen.

The way you develop staff to take on higher levels of responsibility is by creating opportunities to stretch them, encourage risk taking, guide their performance and show confidence in their abilities. Unless you find ways to trust your staff you will not let go to them, and yet how can you trust people if you do not let go.

If you don't bring out the best in others

They may bring out the worst in you

Chapter 7

Get the Best Out of Your Boss

While most managers in the course of a career can expect to attend at least a couple of training sessions on how to manage their staff few can expect even the simplest of guidelines on how to manage upwards. Getting results as a manager doesn't just depend on how well you manage those below you; increasingly it relies on the quality of contacts you build with colleagues and superiors, and the most critical relationship is with your boss. What kind of boss do you have? How well do you manage them and how well do they manage you? Like most people, they have their faults and yet they can be a major part of your support system, as you know if you have ever worked for a really good boss. Alternatively they can become your worst nightmare.

ALLY OR ADVERSARY

The first thing to recognise is that bosses are human – maybe talented, possibly lucky, but human. And their style is often the product of the position in which they find themselves. I remember well my first boss: a hard taskmaster who made impossible demands on his staff while at the same time showing little tolerance for their mistakes. Though he achieved results, it was at great expense to other people, both in individual stress and team spirit. Casualties to his style left the company with a sense of failure, but with a rich store of anecdotes on difficult bosses. His style of managing intrigued me all the more when I visited his home to discover another side to his character: a caring and devoted father to three well-adjusted children and a spouse who called most of the shots. Although I found it hard to understand why he was so different in the office, I find it much easier now.

Bosses are subject to all kinds of pressures that their staff never fully understand. They may have reached their elevated position through technical competence or a time-served apprenticeship to a boss who may have done little to prepare them for managing, and the last thing they need are staff adding to their insecurities. People often make impossible and conflicting demands on their bosses: to be decisive and participative, self-assured and humble, tough and sympathetic as the occasion demands. Their uncertainties we often see as incompetence and their sensitivities as a sign of weakness. We are also slow to appreciate that their bosses may be hounding them for results or that their position isn't quite as secure as the job title or the expense account suggests. It can also be very lonely at the top, where honest feedback is hard to come by, as staff make sure their bosses don't hear too much too often.

Yet, ask any manager for the biggest influences in their career and in nearly every case it includes a present or past boss or mentor as someone who gave them confidence, provided a role model or taught them important lessons the hard way. The plus side of having a good boss is that as an ally, a sounding board or a coach they can satisfy many of our needs for self-development in the job.

Do you have to be lucky to get a good boss? Do you have to make do with the one you've got, or can you do something to get more out of your boss? Yes, you can, and it is probably in your own interests that you do get the best out of your boss; as Peter Drucker confirms, "contrary to popular legend, subordinates don't, as a rule, rise to position and prominence over the prostrate bodies of incompetent bosses". If your boss is a failure it is much more likely that you will be associated with their incompetence than recognised for your own success.

MAKE QUALITY TIME

Short *ad hoc* contacts on job-related issues might lead you to believe that you already see enough of your boss. But, as a manager, do you get enough time to discuss what you are trying to achieve, to solicit the help you need or to raise issues that may be affecting you both? The more pressures in the job the less likely it is you will get quality time, and yet in those circumstances it is even more essential. Just as couples discover the pressures of separate careers or young children can get in the way of family life, so the volume of work can often get in the way of developing relationships with colleagues and bosses. A couple who rented my house a few years ago blocked out an hour each week on a wall chart to discuss family issues and their relationship. While it may appear to stretch the idea of scheduling, people often do make claims for their relationships when even to the most casual observer they are in trouble.

Ask yourself some basic questions about the relationship with your manager.

	Yes	No
Do you know what they want from you?		
Do you get regular feedback on how you are doing?		
Do you know how your performance will be measured?		
Is your boss approachable on problems or issues of concern?		
Are there things you should discuss with your boss but don't?		
Does your boss listen to your views and opinions?		
Do you feel sufficiently recognised for what you do?		
Do the positive interactions with your boss outweigh the negative ones?		

If the answer to most of the above is "no", it may be important to initiate regular meetings with your boss to get them to make time to talk. Why sit around waiting to be appraised, to receive coaching or to get recognition? Demand it, because you need it to be effective. And bosses aren't necessarily the best initiators of discussion about the job. They may have to learn the importance of contact time since they are probably spending less time thinking of you than you are of them.

KEEP THEM IN THE FRAME

If the boss's information about how you are spending your time is sketchy or second hand the risk is they will start to over manage. There is some truth in the maxim that "when people don't understand what is going on the easiest thing is to be obstructionist". A few years ago I had a boss who knew less than I thought about what I was doing. At one annual review he confronted me with negative feedback that he had obviously accumulated over time. Most of it was incorrect and there was little hard evidence to support his claims; but it was about to affect me and our ability to work together. After a couple of head-on meetings where we exchanged views and listened to each other we agreed to meet on a regular two-monthly basis. I took the initiative in arranging those meetings, since it was clearly in my interests that he learned what I was doing through channels that were not selective or distorted. It also gave him an opportunity to talk more openly about his hopes and concerns for the division, so that over a number of meetings I got to know him much better as a person. And there were no more surprises.

Let your boss know frequently what you are doing by sharing your priorities for the month or week, particularly if there is a chance that they may not see things the same way. And your boss is entitled to consider themselves a major source of your priorities; by definition everyone's role in an organisation is to assist the person above them. And don't expect that telling them things once is enough; they need to be reminded about what you are trying to achieve and what you want from them. Only recently I asked a friend where he was spending his holidays this year. He was slightly annoyed that I couldn't remember him telling me about his planned trip to Greece. I apologised, and asked if he remembered where I was going this summer. A smile was enough to confirm that he had forgotten too, although I told him at the same time.

Confirm any agreements you make at meetings with your boss in ways that help to repeat your priorities and your time commitments. Follow up meetings with your boss by sending them a short memo, detailing what was discussed and agreed. Keep restating what may seem obvious to you but not to them. Stan Herman suggests that in any meeting with your boss the "Three Whats" can save you a great deal of unproductive time if used as a guideline.

1. What is the issue or objective?
2. What do you propose?
3. What do you want from the boss?

If you have issues you want to agree with your boss go with options or a solution – preferably in writing. How you present the options or recommendations may depend on the particular boss. Some bosses want a simple proposal, while others expect a more detailed briefing so they can add their own counsel; some want to be told immediately when something has gone wrong, while others want to be briefed only when an issue has been resolved.

TREAT YOUR BOSS AS A CUSTOMER

Would your boss see you as a part of their support system or just another person to manage? For some bosses support means visible commitment to what they are trying to achieve;

for others honest feedback; and for others closeness and availability. Bosses do need to know that you are behind them in whatever way they need to be supported.

One way of supporting your boss is by making time to listen; you could even regard it as part of your job. If your boss is someone who thinks things through by talking them out, then listening may be a significant way of assisting them. Also support your boss by keeping them informed, whether they ask or not. Make a point of giving them information on issues where there is a potential opportunity or threat. Indicate your availability to listen by dropping by occasionally to check how things are with them. As managers frequently monitor their own delegation with a "How are things going?" or "Where are you on that project?", it is easy to assume that bosses do not need that reassurance too.

If you find your boss unsupportive or the relationship less than satisfactory, then it is quite possible that you are both making false assumptions about what one wants from the other. It is easy to end up in a relationship that pleases neither party, as Jerry Harvey's classic parable "The Abilene Paradox" shows only too clearly. The story tells of a grown family who set off one hot and dusty afternoon to drive 53 miles to an uninspiring cafeteria in Abilene. After a meal that one describes as "first-rate material for antacid commercials", the conversation slowly unwinds and it begins to emerge that no one really wanted to go to Abilene; they all went because they thought the others wanted to go.

> *Here we were, four reasonably sensible people who, of our own volition, had just taken a 106-mile trip across a godforsaken desert in furnace-like temperature through a cloud-like dust storm to eat unpalatable food at a hole-in-the-wall cafeteria in Abilene, when none of us had really wanted to go. In fact, to be more accurate, we'd done just the opposite of what we wanted to do.*

It is easy to construct a similar dynamic with your boss, with them assuming your needs and you doing the same, and both being less than satisfied with the outcome. Treating them as a customer means not relying on any one mechanism for providing service but finding many ways to fuel the process, through casual contacts, formal meetings, written comments, passing on information or keeping them updated on your major projects.

One way of reflecting on the quality of your communications is to put yourself in the boss's shoes and ask, "If I were my boss what would I want from me?" Cal Downs and Charles Conrad collected data from over 700 middle managers on just that and found marked differences between staff who were seen as more and less effective by their bosses. Effective subordinates were perceived as more likely to:

- risk confrontation and challenge;
- take the initiative in volunteering their input;
- respond well to downward instructions;
- avoid misunderstanding through checking and feedback;
- state issues factually and thoroughly.

If you want to get more influence with your boss the first thing is to do your homework. You may feel strongly about something but if your boss is undecided you are not going to convince them with opinions. Give your boss convincing data to back your arguments and resist making proposals until you can stand behind them with unassailable facts. In themselves facts are a powerful influencer and yet managers often expect their proposals to be heard without a shred of data to support them. Unsubstantiated opinions leave you open to the challenge to back your proposal with facts, and your boss needs more than opinions if they are to justify your views at another level.

Only recently I listened to the administrator of a hospital facing an angry group of nursing officers who were demanding more staff. She gave a short presentation outlining the key costs and revenues of the hospital, the current staffing levels compared with five years ago and the audited levels of service in each area. She offered no opinions but used the data to show that the hospital was significantly better resourced than five years ago and in receipt of increased net funding over that period. The discussion that followed indicated she had changed a hostile audience into one that was at least prepared to accept the existing resources could be better managed.

TIME-WASTING BOSSES

Sometimes it is difficult for bosses to see how their work-style affects others; usually they are more conscious of the effect their own boss's style is having on them. In a survey of 250 first and second-line supervisors the major complaints about time-wasting bosses stacked up as follows:

1. stopping by to socialise, interrupting priority work;
2. everything that comes up must be done "right now";
3. long meetings at which you weren't needed;
4. priorities being changed midstream;
5. giving assignments that are someone else's responsibility;
6. assignments unclear: incomplete instructions or information;
7. projects given unrealistic timetables;
8. lack of clear authority – boss has to OK everything.

Despite their best efforts, bosses can cause frustration, overwork and stress for managers. Although you may not want to discourage them because you do need their interest, you may want to modify some of their habits. Two strategies for dealing with time-wasting bosses include confronting their behaviours and finding better ways to cope with their style.

Appreciate that your boss may not be completely aware of the problem their habits and idiosyncrasies create for you. It may help them to understand your point of view if you share some data on your major time wasters. Instead of trying to talk them into changing their behaviour, record the amount of your time that was taken up with distractions such as *ad hoc* meetings, queries or paperwork over the last couple of weeks. If they show little interest in changing things at least you know where you stand and if they do show an interest it opens the door for improving the situation.

Also, learn to cope with some of their time-wasting habits – after all, they are the boss and how they choose to manage does matter. Identify particular behaviours that waste your time and find ways to limit the damage. Anticipate some of their interruptions by asking early in the week if there are meetings they want you to attend or issues that require your input. Limit the effect of instant meetings by asking for more regular contacts at times when issues can be raised and dealt with before they become a crisis. Reduce the effects of socialising or interruption by entertaining casual discussion for a limited time, by using discussion enders or visiting them in their office where you have more control on the length of the discussion.

INTOLERABLE BOSSES

All managers have their quirks and we generally learn to manage or cope with them. But what if your manager is nothing but quirks? Those who served under J Edgar Hoover learned that no personal whim could be ignored; even his chauffeurs had to avoid making left turns, after his car was struck by another car while turning left. As a manager he was an erratic autocrat who terrorised subordinates with so many rules and regulations that their adherence to all of them would have been impossible. Even when his instructions were unclear subordinates expected trouble unless they took some form of action without question or query. On reading a note that his secretary was about to release to all field agents Hoover decided he didn't like the layout, so he scribbled a comment at the bottom of the page "watch the borders". As a result FBI agents were placed on special alert all along the Mexican and Canadian borders.

An in-depth survey of 73 highly successful executives found that over three quarters had suffered one intolerable boss in their careers and four had survived two. Most common was the Snake in the Grass who lies, fails to keep their word, compromises their staff and cannot be trusted. The easiest to identify and most difficult to deal with, according to the study, are the Attilas, who are not in the least affected by making wrong decisions themselves but take grave offence if others screw up or shine in any way. Others include the Heel Grinders, who demean their staff, the Egotist, who knows everything, the Dodger, who shirks responsibility, the Incompetent, who does not know what they are doing, the Detail Drone, who goes strictly by the book, the Unrespected Boss and the Slob.

Under the iron fist of Robert Maxwell few of his managers lasted more than a year. Instant decision making, shooting from the hip, outbursts of anger and motivation by fear were all part of a style that stressed key staff like Peter Hassell who left because "I couldn't stand wondering when the stab would come". On one occasion as an assistant pushed a chit in front of Maxwell, he growled, "What's this?" "Approval for a new car for a rep," replied the humbled employee. "Why does he need a new car?" asked the employer as his voice rose to a roar. "Why do we need this man? Fire him".

But, as the survey readily admits, some of the worst bosses were also seen as best in other ways. One manager in the study described his mentor as "a steamroller, mercurial and a total ass", while in an unauthorised biography of Lee Iaccocca one subordinate eulogised him in the words "I never worked for a man I learned more from, admired more – and who was a bigger p***k." Bosses all have strengths and weaknesses, and sometimes their weaknesses are simply the overuse of a strength. What we admire in their decisiveness can at times border on recklessness, their assertiveness on aggression and their commitment on fanaticism. But usually it is not all the person we hate, just bits of them, and it is the bits that we need to confront.

Rather than badmouthing your boss or analysing them in the hope that it will ease the effect, it is more productive to confront them if you are troubled by their behaviour. I recall a teacher friend calling me once in tears. She accused the school principal of being disruptive and deliberately causing her to lose control of the class. It appeared that he had the habit of making unannounced visits to the classroom where he took over the lesson, undermining her confidence to the point where she was thinking of getting out of teaching altogether. After some discussion we agreed that her analysis could be right but that it was worth checking out. A few days later she had an opportunity to confront him and discovered that he had a very high regard for her professionalism. She used the opportunity to tell him how his casual visits were affecting her performance. Although he agreed not to upstage her in future the problem did not completely go away. But it did allow her to see his interventions as enthusiasm rather than criticism and she subsequently found it much easier to cope with his behaviour.

If you have a less than satisfactory relationship with your boss try drawing up a list of their good points. Make them specific and think back to the times you felt particularly happy with your boss. What was going on that isn't happening now? You may be surprised to find the list is longer than you think. Now, identify one or two key things you want to encourage. Brainstorm what you could do to reward them when they do those things and plan to catch them doing at least one thing right each day this week. It could be a very definite "thank you" attached to a specific incident, an invitation to coffee or a compliment within earshot of a colleague.

THE ART OF SUBORDINACY

Most managers were significantly influenced in their careers by someone who supported them, encouraged them to take risks and in whom they were able to confide. A recent study of 520 managers showed that 90 per cent of them recognised a key influencer in their career and for almost half of them that person was an immediate boss.

Making time for managing upwards is a critical part of managing yourself. While most managers acknowledge the importance of managing staff there is increasing evidence that successful managers also build a network of relationships with their peers and senior managers. Less effective managers, by seeing others as an obstacle to doing the job, often deny themselves what they could get from a good boss and from key colleagues, and in doing so, are left unsupported and with little influence.

Although you may not be able to change your boss's personality some aspects of their behaviour can be better understood and managed. Above all, the time you get with your boss should be productive. If you are not getting sufficient quality time, take some responsibility for being better managed. Bosses are not born delegators and mentors. They may think they are communicating, listening and letting go when clearly they are not. If so, it may be important to find ways of relating to them that satisfies their need to feel in control and allows you to get what you want from the relationship. The choice in managing upwards is clear: manage or be managed.

ELEPHANTS & ANTS

Very little in this life can be achieved without the help and support of other people, either your family, friends, colleagues or bosses. Getting support from bosses and colleagues means making time to develop those relationships by treating them as customers, keeping them in the picture and assisting them in return.

But the same people from whom you need support and help can also be one of the major blocks to your achievement if they are wasting your time, changing your priorities or making your job more difficult. Managing results through other people means making time to develop effective relationships with key constituents, and dealing with the fallout that often accompanies our networks with other people.

Putting things off today is the way
We store up problems for the future

Chapter 8

Confront your Indecision and Delay

Sometimes described as "the art of keeping up with yesterday", the habits of delay and indecision are often the result of having difficult choices to make with our time. Indecision is frequently caused by having two equally good alternatives or two equally unpalatable choices to make, so we end up making no choice at all. In the story of the "Imperfect Bride", the cautious suitor makes a list of all the desirable and undesirable characteristics of his long-standing girlfriend only to find an equal number of positives and negatives. Every time he finds something that might tip things in favour of a marriage proposal, another equally convincing negative arrives to restore the balance. Eventually she makes the decision and finds someone else.

> Martin is not untypical of the managers in his company. He gets in at 8.30 am and busies himself for the first half hour checking the computer, voice mail and e-mail and dealing with the daily correspondence. Another half hour is taken up responding to messages and queries from his staff before grabbing a coffee and making his way to a meeting that takes him up to lunch time. The afternoon is similarly packed with a tight agenda – and once again he leaves the office at 6.30 pm with next year's budget in his briefcase as homework. But, instead of getting into it that evening, after a well-earned meal, he slumps into a chair in front of the television, anxious but unable to summon up the energy for a task that he has been putting off for the last two weeks. Will it get done in the same last-minute frenzy as last year?

Why do people procrastinate on some things and then end up doing them in a rush at the last minute? It is a myth that people work best under pressure; most of us work less well when we are anxious, and what excuse do you have if there was a month to get something done and at the last minute you fall sick or lack a vital piece of data? In their anxiety about doing things less than perfectly, some people do not start them at all, or start them too late to ensure that they are done in any other way than badly.

Most procrastination is a response to the stress that accompanies difficult or challenging tasks and, like many stress reactions, it can become a habit and difficult to reverse. Some of the common tasks that suffer from delay and indecision are listed below. Which do you recognise as symptoms of your own procrastination?

* Writing reports or speeches.
* Carrying out performance reviews.
* Confronting difficult people.
* Starting projects.
* Getting things up to date, e.g. filing.
* Doing returns, e.g. budgets, forecasts, tax.
* Reading reports or journals.
* Completing paperwork.
* Filling in forms.
* Chasing people up for things.
* Actioning the outcome of meetings.
* Answering e-mail or voice mail.
* Writing up minutes.
* Asking for resources or assistance.
* Challenging those who waste your time.

Not everyone procrastinates on the same things, which suggests that the habit of delay is a learned response to tasks that may have been stressful in the past; and, like all bad habits, there are things you can do to start unblocking and managing them more effectively. Six useful approaches to tackling procrastination and indecision are easily remembered as the six Ds of delay.

→ Do it.
→ Delegate it.
→ Drop it.
→ Decimate it.
→ Deadline it.
→ Dramatise it.

DO IT

One way to tackle the habit of delay is doing something immediately to break the deadlock. Newton's law of inertia, which suggests that bodies which are at rest tend to remain at rest, equally suggests that bodies which are in motion tend to remain in motion.

Make it the big *A* for today. We often recognise our procrastination in tasks that go from one list to another, or are relegated to the back end of the afternoon. One way to tackle procrastination is to make them a big *A* and commit yourself to getting them off the "to do" list today. Plan to do things on which you delay early in the day and in that way they cease to be a continuing source of anxiety.

Use 10-minute stepping stones. As a way of reducing the anxiety that binds you to delay, commit to spending ten minutes right now to doing something on a difficult task. Take ten minutes to draw up a plan of action for the task or break the task into bits and schedule time for each piece in your diary. Doing ten minutes on something you have been putting off for days is often enough to see the wood for the trees.

Get some data. One major obstacle to getting started on some things is the lack of information to write that report, answer a letter or schedule a job review. Break the back of procrastination today by getting some data on the task: spend half an hour reading a report, sourcing the relevant documents, telephoning a few people for information, printing out some computer files or simply do up a list of the information you need to start the project. Making time to gather information is often enough to feel energised about a task where you feel uncertain or anxious.

DELEGATE IT

One way to rid yourself of things that cause anxiety in your day is to give them to someone else who may find them less stressful and more challenging.

Share your anxiety. If there are things on which you are delaying because you do not like doing them, share your concern with others as a way of getting in touch with your own anxiety: "I hate doing these returns", "I'm really uncomfortable about presenting at that meeting". Not only does sharing a concern help to reduce the anxiety but someone who finds the task less onerous or actually enjoys doing it may volunteer to help you.

Have faith in others. We are sometimes reluctant to give things to our staff because we do not trust their willingness or feel they lack the skills. Yet ask any person about their peak career experiences and for most it was being given something that really stretched them. Most people, when trusted to do something by their boss, will go to great lengths to do it well – as General Patton once said: "Don't tell people how to do things, just tell them what to do and you will be surprised with the results."

Get others to nag. Instead of delegating a difficult task, delegate the monitoring process. One of the best ways to make progress on some things is to let others know that you are trying to finish a report, complete a project, give up smoking or lose weight and get them to frequently remind you about your commitment. In getting this book finished, I have been helped by a couple of friends who regularly asked me: "How is the book going?", "How many chapters have you done?", "When will it be finished?"

DROP IT

Rather than force of habit blocking our progress on difficult tasks, it is often lack of energy that prevents us from getting into the bigger things. Some things are hard to start because there isn't a deadline or a crisis to drive us into action and so it goes from one list to another in the hope that in time we will somehow find the energy to begin.

De-list it. We put some tasks on lists even though we have no real energy to do them. If a task has appeared on a number of your "to do" lists, then one option is to simply cross it off; if it is important it will find a way to get back onto the list in the future when you may have more energy to deal with it. Remember that some things are not worth doing at all and some things are not worth doing right now.

Schedule it for the future. If a particular task is something you want to do but do not have the time or energy right now, one option is to schedule it for the future. If you are under pressure for the next couple of weeks, put a note in your diary to trigger that task at a future date when you are less hassled or likely to see it as another source of anxiety.

Do a worry list. Sometimes putting your concerns on paper is enough to see them differently. After you have drawn up a list of the things on which you have been delaying, consign it to a desk drawer or, better still, put it up on the wall so you can occasionally re-check your concerns. Do a periodic worry list to see that the things you worried about last month were actioned or done in some other way. Also, console yourself with the thought that if you weren't worried about these things you would probably be worried about something else.

DECIMATE IT

Some things we keep putting off because they are big and long term, hard to start and difficult to finish. Most projects have an uncertain beginning because they are unclear and ambiguous and a great deal of energy can be lost during a project if progress is slow or there is no end in sight.

Chunk the elephants. Sometimes big tasks are hard to manage because they demand a time commitment that isn't readily available. One way of dealing with those things is to break them into smaller chunks. Even if you have already broken a project into tasks, break the tasks into even smaller bits as a way of getting started.

> As part of the management team, John had his section of the strategic plan to complete for the next management meeting. He knew it would take a couple of days and, although there was ten days to go, he had been putting it off for the past few weeks. He finally got some momentum into the job by breaking it into bits and picking three small tasks to do tomorrow. He also scheduled four separate hours into his diary to get the bigger chunks completed. Two days later he felt a sense of relief at his progress and much more energy for the challenge.

Breaking things into small chunks often makes them easier to action; it also allows you to get a number of small successes rather than one big success; and short-term successes create and sustain energy to go on to tackle the more difficult chunks of larger projects.

Clock the hours. One way to break the inertia on big tasks is to chunk them into hours and work to the clock. When author James Thurber was finding it difficult to put pen to paper, his long-suffering wife Althea encouraged him to set an alarm clock to ring in 45 minutes and to force himself to have something written by the time it went off – he did and it cured his writers' block. Many things get done if you treat them as a series of time commitments and plan to get something done in each hour.

Figure 8.1: Time Planner

If there is a major task you have been avoiding, make a start by identifying the amount of time you need to give each week to ensure its completion by the deadline. Set a specific goal and, as you complete an hour or half an hour, record it against the goal.

Goal: 6 hours a week for next 6 weeks on XYZ project

Weeks	1	2	3	4	5	6
Hours	✔	✔	✔	✔	✔	✔
	✔	✔	✔	✔	✔	✔
	✔	✔	✔	✔	✔	✔
	✔	✔	✔	✔	✔	✔
		✔	✔	✔	✔	✔
			✔	✔	✔	
			✔		✔	
			✔		✔	
Total	**4**	**5**	**8**	**6**	**8**	**5**

Schedule your procrastination for peak hours. Do things on which you tend to delay at times of the day when you have your best energy. For the average person that is early on in the day – between 8.00 am and 11.00 am for 85 per cent of managers. Apart from getting an early success, you will also be working on the difficult things at times of the day when you have most energy. Leaving difficult things until the back end of the day or taking them home in a briefcase simply adds to the stress by trying to do them when you are most likely to see them as onerous jobs.

Identify a couple of tasks you have been postponing for the past few weeks; it could be a budget proposal, writing a report or dealing with a difficult issue. Use your diary to schedule an hour or two for them this week in your peak time. Although scheduling them into your peak energy hour is no guarantee of success, at least you will be giving them your best shot by attacking them when you have your best mental energy. And a couple of concentrated hours on most major tasks is usually enough to see them as more manageable.

DEADLINE IT

Most projects become troublesome because our energy starts to wane half way through – many people who succeed in life, whether athletes, writers or entrepreneurs, simply persist a little longer.

Use mini-deadlines. While putting a completion date on a project gives you a target to aim for, it is usually too far in the future to provide any immediate energy, the reason that many people wait for an impending deadline to spur them into action. It helps to make energy for deadlines if you break them into bits and put a mini-deadline on each part of the project.

How do major projects get to be late – one day at a time.

Tom Peters

Make deadlines visible by putting them in your diary or on the wall as a reminder of your commitment, and use mini-deadlines to move you on to the next stage, even if you haven't completed the current stage. Aiming for perfection usually means that projects drif, whereas meeting the deadline, even if not to your satisfaction, gives you a sense of success and usually there is time to go back on the bits you need to tidy up.

When I was doing a research degree some years ago, my supervisor was at a university 400 miles away. It took a plane, two train journeys and a taxi to get from where I lived to our six-weekly meetings. Between each visit I worked long and hard to justify the expense and time involved in each trip so that it would not be a wasted

> journey. If we had lived a couple of miles apart we would probably have met more frequently but there would also have been far less need to achieve the kind of progress that was generated by those six-weekly deadlines.

Monitor tasks with mini-events. It helps to break the cycle of under-achievement on projects if you cut them into chunks and find a way to recognise your progress on each chunk. Mini-events might include making a short progress presentation to your peers, rewarding yourself with a break or, better still, rewarding someone like your spouse or staff if you come in on time with a stage of the project.

DRAMATISE IT

Some tasks are put on the long finger because they are boring, routine or seemingly endless. One way to generate some energy for those kind of jobs is to make them more challenging and fun.

Chunk the boredom. While some jobs are neither urgent nor important, they still have to be done. But because they are boring, we often let paperwork or filing pile up on the desk until it becomes a time-consuming and frustrating task.

One way of dealing with routine or boring jobs is to chunk the boredom into half-hour segments. Schedule two half-hour slots this week to clear your desk of paperwork, preferably in the afternoons. Do an occasional blitz on your filing by letting it pile up for a couple of weeks and scheduling two hours each month to get it up to date. Try sorting your paperwork into three files, urgent, important and routine. Read the routine pile once and do something with it – preferably file it in the bin. Schedule some time in the future to deal with the important paperwork and put the urgent stuff on your "to do" list for today.

Make boring tasks into games. Most games are fun because they contain an element of challenge. A woman who hates doing housework starts her day by inspecting the house and putting post-it notes in areas that require her attention. As she completes each task she removes the note and puts it on her kitchen notice board – the challenge is to see how many notes she can collect before her deadline to finish at 11.00 am. Similarly, one successful female executive has a flip chart in her office and a series of post-it notes on the left-hand side with the jobs she has to complete that day. As she completes each task she moves the note to the right side of the board, letting herself and others see the progress she is making.

> I once saw a couple of labourers fixing parking buffers in a car park. The buffers were short slabs of concrete fixed to the tarmac surface with two metal spikes. The two labourers had made a boring job into a game by timing each other hammering the spikes into the ground; and I am sure they had more than a gentleman's wager on the result.

Make your procrastination into fun. Some things are easier to handle if they are treated in a more light-hearted way. Look at varying the location of your routine meetings as a way of making them more fun – have some standing up, in the canteen or outdoors. Consider having the occasional off-site meeting at a hotel to look at the big picture, and include a break for physical activity or a team challenge.

The management activity that is most subject to procrastination is planning – it tends to go by the board if there is a crisis and much of it gets done outside working hours. One way to get more time for planning is to make it fun: try staying at home one morning a month to review your results and plan for the next period; try more creative approaches to planning, such as doing drawings of the future, having a half-hour brainstorming sessions with a couple of colleagues or taking a thoughtful walk. If you need time to read reports or journals, do it in the park or the lobby of a hotel. Plan things, such as job reviews on train journeys, have planning meetings in a local cafe and hold competitions to get creative ideas for improving service or delivery.

Many things conspire to get in the way of what we are trying to achieve as managers, and foremost among them is ourselves. Although some habits we develop for coping with work overload or anxiety are useful, others only add to our feelings of pressure and under-achievement. While it is sometimes good to delay on things or let your subconscious work on decisions overnight, if it is getting in the way of what you want to achieve in the job, then do something to break the habits that may be feeding your procrastination or look at ways to replace your bad habits with better and more productive routines. Procrastination really is the thief of time.

ELEPHANTS & ANTS

While procrastination is the thief of time, it is also a habit we use to avoid getting into the bigger and more difficult things in the job. If procrastination and indecision are blocking you from achieving what you want to get done, try one of the six strategies for breaking the stranglehold of delay: Do it, Delegate it, Drop it, Decimate it, Deadline it or Dramatise it.

If there is something you want to get done, but have been putting off for a while, try doing something small to break the inertia that accompanies procrastination. Make it into a big A for today, schedule it into your peak energy hour or treat it as a baby elephant by breaking it into smaller and more manageable pieces. Don't delay, do something now.

By colluding in daily time wasters and distractions

We avoid the results we are trying to achieve

Chapter 9

Minimise the Daily Distractions

Although managing time means making better choices and focusing on the real challenges in the job, a lot of things get in the way of what managers want to get done with their day. Apart from the work they should be giving away to others and the tasks that are subject to procrastination, managers also have to deal with a volume of time wasters that come at the rate of one every seven minutes and account for upwards of 20–30 per cent of their time – one day in every week.

TOP TEN TIME WASTERS:
RANK ORDER (220 MANAGERS)

- Telephone.
- Saying "no".
- Day-to-day crises.
- Having to chase others up.
- Drop-in visitors.
- Personal disorganisation.
- Being too available.
- Procrastination.
- Correspondence and paperwork.
- *Ad hoc* and regular meetings.

Not only do managers spend a substantial amount of their time dealing with daily distractions but the cumulative effect of those minor derailments, which may only take a few minutes here or there, can add up to a major block to getting the important tasks done.

COLLUSION AND CURE

A few illuminating comments on the nature of time wasters helps to recognise them for what they are.

1. You cannot eliminate time wasters altogether because many of them go with the job. But to manage effectively you do need to minimise the effect of constant distractions, such as the telephone or drop-ins.

2. At best managers collude in their time wasters. They learn to live in an atmosphere that is characterised by telephone interruptions and minor crises and would miss many of them if they were absent – wouldn't it be a dull old day if the telephone never rang or there was no correspondence or drop-in visitors? Be honest.

3. Not only do managers collude in their time wasters, they encourage some of them as a way of avoiding the more important tasks. How often have you dropped into someone's office as a way of avoiding a job that was sitting on your desk that you did not want to start? How often have you allowed yourself to be sidetracked by the easy things on your "to do" list as a way of avoiding the ones you know are more difficult?

4. Managers blame many of their time wasters on other people. "Attribution Theory" suggests that the human condition is to blame our failures on others and to claim successes for ourselves. Many managers who complain about the volume of telephone interruptions in their day also carry a mobile phone everywhere they go, respond immediately and encourage others to call them on the slightest pretext. Managers who complain about the number of drop-ins frequently have an open-door policy, comfortable chairs to encourage the sitters and body language which suggests that casual visitors are more than welcome to interrupt.

Of course some time wasters are in the nature of the job or part of the culture of doing business – or are they? If, as a manager, you are spending an inordinate amount of time dealing with distractions and minor issues in the day then you are probably not achieving what you are there to achieve. While you may be inclined to blame others for wasting your time you also have to accept some responsibility for colluding in them and start to take ownership for minimising their effects.

CHRONIC TIME WASTERS

Breaking out of time-wasting habits is not easy because many of them, like long hours or taking work home, are chronic, and chronic habits are hard to break. And most managers have already tried the usual prescriptions for dealing with their time wasters and found they have not worked. Rather than steeling yourself to remedies that have failed in the past, you need to start looking for creative ways to break the habits that waste your time.

One simple process for identifying creative solutions to chronic time wasters is brainstorming, which has three simple rules.

1. Take five minutes to list all the creative solutions you can think of to one of your major time wasters. As well as the practical solutions, also look for the wild or extreme possibilities. (Try it as a group exercise on a shared time waster, such as meetings or paperwork – two or three heads are more creative than one.)

2. Do not edit what you write down. Put everything on the list no matter how ridiculous it may seem.

3. Now pick the most "practical idea" from the list and the "wildest idea". Although the practical idea may seem more likely to succeed, often the wildest idea presents the seed of a better solution. At a recent brainstorming session, one of the suggestions for dealing with telephone interruptions was to put the phone in a bucket of water. The idea of cooling down the phone suggested taking it off the hook for an hour each day, getting away from it if there is something you want to finish or rotating the handling of telephone queries so that everyone takes a turn.

At all levels, there are creative ideas that suggest solutions to chronic time wasters. As CEO of IBM, Frank Carey cut down the amount of time taken up at meetings with ill-conceived proposals by insisting that all proposals were expressed on a single sheet of paper. A senior manager in a small company who spends two days a week away from the office found that his staff had developed the convenient habit of leaving their problems on his desk on pieces of paper. He often came back to the office to find a minor mound of paper that contributed little to his effectiveness. His solution was to remove his desk from the office so that people had no place to leave the paper. And it worked so well that he introduced a paperless office – the rule was that no piece of paper came into his office without going out again.

Faced with the problem of winter icing on cables, which was costing a fortune in repairs and seriously affecting customer service, a North American electricity supplier used brainstorming to come up with ideas for resolving the issue. One of the wild ideas was to string pots of honey along the cables to encourage hungry bears to climb the pylons and in so doing to dislodge the ice. Further visions of "a bear in the air" lead to the possibility of using the down draft of a helicopter to dislodge ice from the cabling. That relatively simple solution ended up saving thousands of dollars a year for the company in reduced repairs and unbroken service.

As you examine the solutions to your major time wasters be aware of your own tendency to dismiss the more creative and imaginative ideas with phrases such as "It wouldn't work" or "I couldn't get away with that". Killing off creative ideas (ideacide) is one of the ways in which we deny possibilities for improving things – in the same way that insurance companies condemned customers to a lengthy application process until someone came up with the idea of direct telephone sales, or that caused mainframe computer companies to dismiss the PC as a crazy idea until someone saw otherwise.

CREATIVE SOLUTIONS

At the risk of adding to the list of handy hints for resolving time wasters, here are some creative solutions for minimising the more common distractions in your day.

Detach yourself from the Phone

Without doubt, the biggest disrupter in the day is the telephone. With its insistent ring and potential for surprise, most people cannot resist answering the phone even if they are in the middle of something much more important. No matter how long the line in a bank or airline office the telephone gets precedence – at meetings serious issues are set aside while someone rushes from the room to take the most trivial of calls on their mobile. On a recent television chat show one of the guests even interrupted the interviewer to take a call from her mother.

One way of reducing the invasiveness of the telephone is by logging the content and duration of your calls over two to three days – you may find that many of them could have been redirected or handled in a shorter time. Have a "quiet time" in the day when you are not willing to be interrupted. In the same way that some companies have introduced dress down days, why not have a telephone free morning, a few hours in the week when all internal calls are banned and voice-mail messages are taken for external calls.

Start to reply to calls at times of the day when you expect to get the other person's voicemail; it will ensure they get the message and the call will be brief. Use the 20/80 principle on calls – decide who you want to receive calls from and get a message on the others. Finally, if you cannot hide the interruptions, then hide yourself. Work in someone else's office for the couple of hours you need for thinking or planning, or start working from home one day a month to write reports or do a blitz on your reading.

Say "No" and Mean It

Why do people say "yes" to things and then later regret it? Partly, it is to avoid the guilt that goes with saying "no", even if it is at great expense to our own work. Also, it is because most people have difficulty saying "no" to things that are in the future – if someone wants to meet or visit you next month you are much more likely to say "yes" than if the same person wanted to meet with you right now.

At a practical level, it is much easier to say "no" if you are certain about what you want to get done with your own time. Having the clear focus of long-term priorities, a "to do" list and scheduled diary commitments on major tasks makes it much easier to fend off the time stealers. It is also easier to say "no" if you practice being assertive, using "I" statements, such as "I'm sorry but I have to finish this by 4.00 pm", while at the same time making eye contact and using body language that is forceful.

Draw up a list of the things on which you want to start saying "no" and record your success. Before making commitments to others, give yourself a breathing space by sleeping on it overnight – a good night's rest is often enough to convince you to say "no" to something that could so easily have wasted your time. Pick a role model who is assertive with their time and adopt a couple of their habits. Punish people who dump their problems on you by sending them away with one of yours and hounding them for a response. Reward yourself for saying "no" and make the reward unusual, such as a trip to an art gallery or buying a new pair of shoes or, alternatively, just stop responding to some people so quickly or at all – get a reputation for not being a soft touch.

Reduce the Daily Crises

Day-to-day crises usually take the form of minor problems from a variety of sources including your boss, staff, colleagues or customers. Most of them aren't novel, they have happened before and as such lend themselves to being made into procedures or delegated. As minor crises on aeroplanes or at theme parks are handled by the most junior of staff, get the pleasure of watching your staff taking responsibility for the crises and reward them as an encouragement to continue their efforts.

Also, reward others, such as your boss, for going to your staff in the first instance: "You will find Jim is the real expert in this area." And when a problem comes onto your desk the first question you should always ask is: "Why me?" Before responding to any issue consider whether it is urgent or whether someone else could do it – most crises aren't that critical and could probably be handled by a number of people. If it has to be handled by you, then see it as an opportunity to deal with things differently in the future – train others in crisis handling or start to monitor issues that have a potential for becoming problems in the future.

Control your Chasing Up

One of the consequences of relying on others is the amount of chasing up you may have to do to get them to meet their deadline. Managers often compound the problem by doing urgent things themselves or establishing a norm that things are not urgent until they have reminded people at least a couple of times.

One of the best ways to get others to deliver on time is to nag them, either by confronting the individual whenever you see them, grabbing them first thing in the morning, sitting in their office until you get an answer or delegating the "nagging" to someone else who may get a better response.

When Alan Ladd Jnr was at United Artists he wanted to re-employ a technician on a consultancy basis. Ladd was being put through the usual difficulties by personnel and wanted his boss to put pressure on them to make a decision, but with little success. Before he left on a two week business trip he dictated fourteen memos to his secretary with the instruction that she should send one of them to his boss each day with the same request: "Have you got the decision yet?" At the end of his travels he came back to a positive response.

Use reverse psychology, praising those who deliver on time, or alternatively stop nagging the worst offenders and let a crisis occur so they can see that you are not going to chase them up every time.

Discourage the Drop Ins

People who waste your time with casual or frequent interruption are not too much of a problem unless there is something more important on your desk. But instead of telling them to go away, we often collude in their disruptions with an open door and an absence of feedback that might indicate they are less than welcome. As a result we often end up working late to get something done that we could have got done in the day.

Try using discussion enders to bring casual conversations to a close: "Is that it?" or "Was there something else?" And if that doesn't work try being more assertive: "I have to get this in the post by lunch time" or just walk out of the room and leave them sitting. If it is your boss who keeps interrupting, think of regularising a weekly meeting or touching base at a time in the day that suits you. Also, let them know how things are going before they ask – they are entitled to know if something they delegated is being done or has run into trouble. If you are undertaking a project for your boss give them regular progress reports so they know you are on schedule and won't be embarrassed if someone asks how the project is going.

If your staff are the main interrupters, adopt the policy of not accepting their "monkeys" – send them away to do some thinking rather than giving them a solution which may encourage them to keep coming back. Get them to put the problem in writing or assure them of your support in whatever they decide and keep letting them know the problem is theirs, not yours. Also, regularise daily or weekly meetings so that issues can be left until the next meeting rather than encouraging them to drop in at inconvenient times of the day.

Have a closed-door policy for part of the day – hide somewhere people are less likely to get hold of you or put a notice on your door for an hour saying: "Do Not Disturb" and do not add "please", which makes it conditional on the person deciding whether the interruption is important enough.

GETTING TO GRIPS WITH THE ANTS

Time wasters are hard to tackle because many of them go with the job. They are also part of the buzz of working in organisations and, as such, create variety for managers who like them all the more for that. In certain cases, time wasters can also be used as work avoidance techniques (WATS) providing managers with a convenient cover for things they are reluctant to start.

Managing time wasters isn't so much a question of eliminating all the distractions in your day but minimising them – at times you may have little alternative but to answer the phone or to drop everything and handle a crisis. But, if the ants continue to prevent you from achieving what you want to get done in the day then you do have to find ways to control them.

As a strategy for breaking the habits that may be feeding your time wasters the following approaches can help.

1. **Make sure you keep focused on the elephants**. If you have daily and weekly priorities for which you are making time it is much easier to let go of the habits that sustain your time wasting.

2. **Identify the main time leaks in the job**. Get in touch with the things that frustrate your efforts, the interruptions that tend to fragment your day or the tasks that take up your time and contribute little to your effectiveness. If a particular time waster accounts for a chunk of the problem, then get some data on the number of interruptions, their duration and impact. Set a goal to reduce the time you spend on specific time wasters and have an action plan for implementing it.

3. **Replace some of your bad habits with good habits**.
   Reduce the number of minor crises or interruptions from
   your staff by having regular meetings or monthly one on
   ones. Replace the habit of allowing the telephone to
   interrupt you on important tasks by completing those tasks
   away from the phone or at lunch time. Have a quiet time in
   the day when you let the answer machine take messages –
   even leave a recorded message so people will know when you
   are available.

4. **Look for more creative ways to reduce the time wasters**.
   Recognise that the remedies you have already tried aren't
   working and you need to do something different, preferably
   more creative, on the basis that most habits are chronic.
   Many companies have adopted creative approaches to some
   of the more common time wasters by having stand-up
   meetings, insisting on one-page memos, having an hour of
   quiet time in the day and establishing dress down days. The
   unusual is now becoming a more acceptable way for
   managers to work.

Managing the ants doesn't mean eliminating everything that
gets in the way of your effectiveness – some time wasters
should be enjoyed for what they are – opportunities to reflect,
a break from the routine or a chance to network with
colleagues. However, getting to grips with the time robbers does
mean changing your locus of control away from believing there
is nothing you can do to influence them to recognising that you
can minimise their effect. Some things in the day have to be
done but not to the extent that we end up doing them. Some
time wasters are a choice – to be available, to procrastinate, to
set unrealistic time estimates and to entertain drop-ins.

Managing the time wasters in your day also means learning
to be more ruthless if you really want to make progress on the
important things in your job – start to take a bit more
responsibility for controlling the things that can so easily end
up controlling you.

ELEPHANTS & ANTS

While you cannot eliminate time wasters altogether, as many of
them go with the job, you do need to find ways to minimise
them, otherwise the ants can easily overwhelm the elephants

in your day. The difficulty with the routine time wasters like the telephone or e-mail is that we learn to live with them and would miss them if they were gone. And in the same way as habits like smoking or overeating, most time wasters are chronic in the sense that you have already tried the normal remedies and failed. Chronic time wasters demand creative solutions, something unusual that you have not tried before, and preferably something more imaginative. Brainstorm some creative solutions to one of your major time wasters today and pick one or two ideas to action. Remember: if what you are doing now is not working then try something else.

Beating your way out of work pressure

Only adds to the stress you are trying to avoid

Chapter 10

De-stress the Work Pressure

Managing time is about making wise choices, to focus on the elephants and finding ways to manage the ants. But making difficult choices isn't easy or relaxing – give a child a bar of chocolate and they will eat it, give them the choice of one thing in the sweet shop and they are immediately showing signs of stress. Much of the stress at work comes from the way that managers react to the many difficult and often confusing choices in the job – while some respond to the daily pressures in the job by making better choices with their time others try to beat their way out of pressure and over commitment by working even longer hours to catch up with the increasing backlog.

EU-STRESS AND DISTRESS

Not all stress is bad. Eu-stress ("eu" stands for euphoria) is the kind of stress that leads people to peak performance, helps them respond to crises and adapt to change, and some managers need more of it in the job. But the negative side of stress, which we mainly recognise in ourselves, is the result of a continuous and unrelenting pressure that pushes us beyond our ability to adapt and leads to anxiety, exhaustion and sometimes burnout.

The Job Stressors

Some stress comes from the type of jobs we have and some from the kind of people we are. The most common job stressors include:

- continuous and tight deadlines;
- job overload;
- long hours;
- fire fighting rather than working to a plan;
- role ambiguity and conflict;
- inadequately trained staff;
- constant negative feedback.

A great deal of the job stress that managers experience can be summed up in one word, "overwork". Under constant pressure to improve results against increasing competition and limited resources, the 2-3-2 formula suggests that in today's environment half the people are doing three times the work for twice the pay. One recent survey shows that two out of every five managers are working more than 50 hours a week and one in eight are doing more than 60 hours, not including travel or taking work home. The pressure on people to work longer and harder is further reflected in a recent survey of UK office workers which found that 25 per cent take a lunch break of less than 30 minutes, 20 per cent regularly skip their lunch and 2 per cent go without lunch altogether.

The Personality Stressors

While stress comes from the types of job we do, it also comes from the kind of people we are and the way we respond to pressures in the job. In a classic study on stress and personality, Drs Roseman and Friedman looked at 3,500 healthy men and their response to stress conditions. On the basis of their lifestyle and ways of coping with pressure, the researchers classified them as *Type A* and *Type B* personalities, and predicted that the *Type A*s would suffer more heart attacks than *Type B*s. Over the ten year period of the study 250 of the group suffered coronaries of whom 85 per cent were *Type A* personalities.

Type A	Type B
Very competitive	Not competitive
Strong, forceful	Easy-going manner
Does everything quickly	Methodical
Ambitious	Moderately ambitious
Impatient	Not upset by delays
Very conscious of time	Not conscious of time
Restless when inactive	Enjoys periods of inactivity

While *Type A* managers are go-getters, intolerant of delays, always ready to assume responsibility and tend to work better when they are up against tight deadlines, the *Type B*s tend to be more placid, task oriented and slower to anger. Although most people are a mixture of both types, many successful managers would tend towards a *Type A* personality.

SYMPTOMS AND CAUSES

Whether you are working in a stressful environment or have to live with a stressful personality, it isn't so much the pressure that causes the problems but the way you respond. Some useful habits for coping with pressures at work are suggested by examining three broad strategies for dealing with stress: recognising the symptoms, reducing the daily effects of time pressure and removing the root causes.

Recognise the Symptoms

Organisational life does not cause stress, just stress conditions. When people first experience the effects of continuous work pressure, they often dismiss the symptoms as temporary, expecting them to disappear when the pressure is relieved, or they disguise them with self-medication, alcohol or coffee. When the symptoms re-appear, the tendency is to rationalise them as part of the job or to see them as personal weaknesses rather than as warning signals of a longer term condition. Left unchecked, the initial signals of stress can lead to more persistent and pernicious conditions, such as hypertension and arthritis, and other serious diseases which research is only beginning to link with stress, such as asthma, diabetes and cancer.

INITIAL STRESS SIGNALS

Physical	**Emotional**
Fatigue	Anxiety
Sleep problems	Feeling of being out of control
Muscle aches	Withdrawal from others
Indigestion	Loss of concentration
Headaches	Inability to relax
Palpitations	Loss of self-worth
Skin rashes	Concern about health

Figure 10.1: Stress Facts

- A CBI Survey shows 30–40 per cent of absences from work are due to stress.

- 90 million days are lost each year in the UK through stress.

- Stress is costing the EU €20 billion annually. A recent report suggests one in three workers is stressed by lack of control in the job.

- In Sweden, the cost of heart disease due to stress is 3,190 million ECU.

- One in twenty workers suffers from depressive illnesses in Ireland.

- In the US over $295 million worth of tranquillisers is consumed each year and $195 million is spent on sleeping pills.

While stress is mainly associated with the negative side of work pressure, it is also associated with success. Executive "burnout", which is defined as the accumulation of stress over time, shows no obvious symptoms in the short term, but in the long term can leave its victims psychologically disabled with feelings of anger, helplessness, of being trapped in the job, disillusioned with their careers and putting increasing effort into maintaining the hectic pace they have set for themselves. According to Dr Freudenberger, who popularised the concept of "burnout", the typical candidate is "dynamic, charismatic and goal-oriented", a pretty accurate description of many successful managers.

Figure 10.2: How Burned Out Are You?

How often do these things apply to you?
seldom=1, sometimes=2, often=3, very often=4

I do not feel rested or relaxed	
I feel no sense of accomplishment	
I worry about the future	
I feel trapped	
My work is not interesting	
I have poor communications with others	
There is never enough time to do things correctly	

Figure 10.2: How Burned Out Are You? (contd)

The work is just too hard

I get no support from others

My co-workers are always complaining

I ache and feel less than well

I regret lost opportunities

I have no sense of direction

I have low self-esteem

My co-workers are unco-operative

Total

Interpretation of the scores

54–60: burned out

44–53: likely to burn out

34–43: initial symptoms of burn out

24–33: OK

15–23: doing fine

Reduce the Daily Stressors

While the more traditional approaches to stress management emphasise removing the causes of work pressure or changing your job conditions, others focus on reducing the daily effects of working in a stressful environment. When you feel harassed, under pressure or out of control in the day, rather than trying to beat your way out of it, do something to relieve the effects.

Take a breather. When people are anxious they often take short and shallow breaths. Not only does this restrict their oxygen supply but it also results in an increase of carbon dioxide to the bloodstream, constricts the blood vessels, reduces oxygen supply to the brain and adds to feelings of tension and panic. One simple way to relieve anxiety during the day is to take three or four deep breaths whenever you feel anxious, drawing in as much air as you can, and as you exhale saying the word "relax", silently. By focusing on your body you take the tension off your mind.

Have frequent stretch breaks. When they are under pressure, people often experience tightening of the muscle endings which results in unspecific aches and overall body stiffness. Taking a stretch break every hour, by tightening up and loosening each muscle in turn, can help relieve those symptoms. Start by pulling your toes towards your knees and holding it for the count of ten. Feel the tension in the backs of your legs. Now, relax and feel the tension go. Do the same with your thighs and so on up to your face opening your mouth wide and stretching your chin as far as it will go to the count of ten. Feel the tension disappear and then relax for a few minutes.

Take a nap. Many well-known figures have found that taking a short nap is a convenient antidote to daily fatigue. Celebrity nappers have included Albert Einstein, John Kennedy and Winston Churchill, while Billy Graham always takes a nap before an important speech and Mark McCormack, business adviser to famous sportsmen, schedules a lunch time rest as a daily commitment. In support of the afternoon nap, physiologists have recently discovered that the body's natural energy goes through a marked dip in the middle of the day, suggesting that the siesta cultures, such as Greece and Mexico, have probably got things right.

> According to legend, the painter Salvador Dali took frequent naps during the day. To make sure that he didn't fall into a deeper sleep he sat in a chair, his arm hanging down with a spoon cupped loosely between his fingers. Underneath the spoon, on the floor, was a tin plate. By the time the spoon hit the floor he had dozed just enough to be refreshed by the rest.

Try a power walk. If you are tired after lunch or are in the habit of sinking into a chair after a heavy evening meal get into the routine of going for a brisk twenty minute walk instead. Apart from aiding digestion, a brisk walk can help to normalise blood pressure and reduce cholesterol. Power walking simply means walking at a pace that increases the metabolic rate (consumption of calories) and the heart rate, about two steps every second, the pace of a moderate hand clap.

Remove the Root Causes

Most persistent stress conditions are the result of a steady build up of fatigue over time. On the basis that managing is a hazardous profession, it is sound advice for any manager to keep in good physical shape and one of the most effective ways is regular exercise.

Practice aerobic fitness. Meaning "in the presence of oxygen", aerobic fitness requires regular exercise, at least twice a week, sufficient to increase the intake of oxygen for at least twenty minutes. The effects of aerobic exercise can be achieved through a standard workout programme or any aerobic sport, such as cycling, tennis, jogging, swimming or brisk walking. Most important is that you exercise in a way that you enjoy rather than making it another task to be squeezed into your busy day.

It also helps if you make a regular commitment to exercise by joining a class, block out specific times in your diary for exercise, involve others in the activity or keep a chart of your progress. You can add direction to any exercise programme by making it into a challenge, such as planning to run a mini-marathon, doing a sponsored walk or placing a bet on reducing your weight. Another way of committing to healthy exercise is to replace some of your bad habits with good ones, such as scheduling a weekly tennis game, going for a swim or having a gym session straight after work as a way of encouraging you to leave the office on time.

Keep in good mental shape. Originally developed by the Maharishi Yoga as transcendental meditation (TM) the "relaxation response" was popularised among the business community by Dr Herbert Benson. It involves two twenty-minute sessions a day in which a mantra (silent sound) is repeated as a way of calming the racing thoughts that frequently accompany anxiety and fatigue. The five steps in the relaxation response are simple and unmystical.

1. Sit in a comfortable position.
2. Close your eyes.
3 Relax your muscles one by one starting at your feet and progressing to your face. Allow them to remain relaxed.
4. Breathe through your nose and become aware of your breathing. As you breathe out say the word "one", silently to yourself and continue saying "one" at each outward breath.
5. Continue to relax for twenty minutes and when you have finished, sit quietly for a couple of minutes.

In an experiment on the benefits of the relaxation response, 80 subjects with high blood pressure were asked to meditate for twenty minutes twice a day over a nine-week period. During the experiment, their systolic and diastolic pressures fell by an average of ten millimetres, bringing them down to normal levels. Equally interesting was that those who stopped meditating after the experiment found their blood pressure soon returned to its original level.

Eat early and snack often. Many of the problems associated with fatigue and anxiety relate to poor diet. We are all familiar with the harassed manager, on the go from early morning until late evening, consuming numerous cups of coffee, snacking on biscuits and lunching on the run. According to Dr Michael McGannon, Medical Director at INSEAD and author of *The Urban Warrior*, battling the effects of dietary fatigue should include elements of the following action plan.

1. Go for a brisk 15-minute walk after lunch.
2. Do not mix proteins and starches, which are incompatible foods.
3. Avoid alcohol at lunch time.
4. Snack sensibly between meals, e.g. nuts, cheese, and fruit, to avoid low sugar levels.
5. Limit your coffee intake.
6. Drink two to three litres of fresh water daily – between meals.

Contrary to the myth that coffee and sugar increase your energy during the day, they can actually add to fatigue by over stimulating the adrenal glands which in turn leads to a rush of insulin and premature fatigue. The same applies to sweets or biscuits which may give you a temporary lift for about an hour but will leave you with less energy in the longer term. Also important for avoiding fatigue is that you consume most of your high energy food in the first half of the day – instead of a light breakfast of toast, cereal and coffee, the traditional breakfast that includes sugar and fat to slow down digestion is still the best. And try to avoid eating late in the evening, which is likely to reduce your ability to get a good night's sleep. The old adage "breakfast like a king, lunch like a prince and dine like a pauper" still remains pretty sound advice.

Let go of perfection. The people most susceptible to stress in the workplace are the perfectionists who want to get everything done, do not trust others and treat everything as if it were urgent and important. Perfectionists are hard on themselves, punishing their own imperfections by working harder to get everything right and denying others opportunities to relax and enjoy their work. If your perfectionism is denying you time for relaxation or enjoyment, then try to build in a few good habits to replace those which are adding to your stress.

1. Start walking to work, or part of the way, or go walking at lunch time.
2. Plan two weekend breaks with your family.
3. Delegate one job or family responsibility to someone else.
4. Track the hours you put into the job and plan to reduce them.
5. Learn to trust others by scheduling more time with your key staff.
6. Set a deadline on starting and finishing meetings – set a time limit on tasks (not everything is worth doing well).
7. Have a quiet time or twenty-minute nap in the day.
8. Set aside half an hour once or twice a week to read – do it in a relaxing place like a coffee shop or a park bench.
9. Have lunch with a colleague or friend at least once a week.
10. Keep a diary to reflect and plan to do things differently.

Managing is a hazardous profession. Unlike the doctor, lawyer or teacher, a manager's success cannot be measured in the number of clients they see or the hours they spend in the classroom. They are evaluated against the results they achieve, which are often ambiguous, long term and considerably outside their control. The danger for managers is believing that if you work harder and longer there is more chance of being effective or successful in the job. Working hard is no guarantee of success in managing – much more critical is identifying where you want to go for the future and focusing on the priorities while at the same time recognising "busyness" as one of the major blocks to effectiveness.

Managing effectively means making better choices with your time, not trying to do everything right but doing the right things right. Not only does focusing on everything mean that you are focusing on nothing, it is also a recipe for long hours, frustration and stress. While managers do need occasional bouts of pressure to experience the euphoria of beating a deadline or handling a crises, if that pressure becomes the norm, it can lead to levels of distress that are debilitating in the short term and, in the long term, may contribute to a more permanent condition.

While stress may go with the job of managing, it is how you deal with the pressure that makes all the difference. Recognise the symptoms of your stress as convincing data for change, find ways to relieve the daily work pressures and plan to remove the longer term causes – you cannot kill time but it can end up killing you.

ELEPHANTS & ANTS

Working hard is hard work, achieving things is energising. If you are experiencing the negative symptoms of stress, don't ignore them until they become a major issue – start to do things differently. On the basis that managing is a stressful profession, build things into your day to relieve the pressure, such as taking a twenty minute walk at lunchtime, having stretch breaks when you feel tense, or taking short naps.

Longer term preventative measures include regular exercise, a good diet, regulating your working hours, examining your work style and building breaks into the year. Start to manage the pressures in the job rather than choosing to become a victim to them

If you identify with success it identifies with you

Identify with failure and you will succeed – at failing

Chapter 11

Start to Make it Happen

Do you ever consider how some people achieve so much in their lives while others barely manage to survive? Do you wonder why some people make things happen while others have things happen to them? Have you ever puzzled why some people are so successful in their careers and yet so unfulfilled in their personal lives? Although we attribute personal or job success to traits such as confidence, talent, money or charisma, most people who succeed in life do things to plan for their success and make time to work the plan: as the words of a recent song suggest: "It's not what you've got, it's what you do with what you've got."

PLAN FOR SUCCESS

Rather than lacking time to be effective, what most managers lack is direction and energy in the job. While there are other avenues for getting direction, one place to start is with your ambitions and aspirations. Although you may feel that your job is to manage the day-to-day work and to get results, you are also there to make things happen for the future, to change things, to develop things and to introduce new ideas – it is the leadership part of your function.

> Write a short letter projecting yourself two years from now: What difference will you have made in your area? What will you have achieved or got done in that period? Underline three things and make them commitments for action in the next six months. Put them up on the wall of your office as a reminder that you are not there just to do things but to achieve and get things done. Diary an appointment with yourself three months from now to review progress on your long-term ambitions.

While most managers are comfortable with planning for today or for this week, they are less convinced about giving time to planning their long-term vision or goals. In the same way that intending couples often give more time to organising the wedding than to planning the marriage, things go wrong for managers because they fail to anticipate and plan for the future; and long-term planning only happens if you make time to think about the business, to have off-site planning days or to set up a planning group.

But having plans is one thing, making them happen is another. Knowing where you are going for the future is important, but you cannot do a vision or a mission because they are too ambiguous and long-term to action. The way to work on your long-term plan is to make those things into challenges and to fuel them with priorities and tasks in the shorter term. Combine your plans for the future with what you want to get done on a daily and a weekly basis to ensure that you are going where you planned to go and to create energy for the journey.

GET MORE BALANCE IN YOUR LIFE

It is a fact that most managers today are working harder and longer hours than they did ten years ago. It is also a reality that many managers are experiencing job-related stress, taking little exercise, eating on the run and neglecting their personal lives.

On a tennis coaching holiday a couple of years ago, I met Peter who, at coffee one morning, began to tell me about a heart attack he had suffered two years earlier. I found it hard to relate to his comment that it was the best thing that had ever happened to him. He explained that working long hours over several years had kept him away from his family to the extent that they did not seem to need or want him. Home had become a less welcoming place and as a result he found even more convincing reasons to stay at the office. Regular visits from his family while he was recovering from triple bypass surgery gave him a second chance to appreciate what he was missing and the resolve to change his lifestyle. From believing that nothing would get done unless he was there to do it, he discovered that his staff were more than capable in his absence. He also came to realise that his job as manager was to provide them with leadership rather than with time.

To remain effective as a manager, it is important to maintain a good balance between your personal and work life. Rather than feeling guilty about the long hours, the time you give to your family, or your lack of exercise, regard them as challenges to succeed in all aspects of your life. The following questions may help to clarify some of your personal aspirations over the next year.

- What are the main challenges in your personal life for the next year: health, family, recreation, spirituality?

- Who is important in your life that you would like to give more time: spouse, children, friends, parents, networks, clubs or societies?

- What childhood ambitions do you still harbour: travel, relationships, hobby or an interest?

- Have you a particular talent or skill you would like to develop: a language, acting, computers, golf, voluntary or public speaking?

- Is there a decision you have put off in the last year that you want to do something about: weight, smoking, relationships, career, lifestyle or education?

- If you had a magic wand what would you change about your lifestyle?

Take five minutes to list down all the things you would like to action in the next six months to get more balance into your life. Now pick two to focus on for the next month. Try making them into clear goals, for example: "Lose 6 lbs by 31 December" or "Plan four weekends away with the family and have two completed by 6 July".

PLAN AHEAD: ACT NOW

There is a big difference between having plans and making them happen. Action plans are no guarantee of action: most never get beyond the wish list stage. If you want to change your approach to your job or personal life you need to treat them as overwhelming tasks, elephants that are best eaten by breaking them into chunks and starting on the easy bits – remember that success breeds energy and energy breeds success. Many managers fail to realise their long-term ambitions or goals not because they lack direction but because they lose energy for the bigger challenges under pressure from the myriad of daily routines and minor problems.

If you seriously want to improve the way you manage your time, do not put this book down until you have resolved to do something in the next two weeks to start the process – remember, any long journey begins with a single step.

As a first step to improving your time management pick three things from the list below that you will absolutely commit to doing in the next two weeks.

- Start going home earlier in the evenings at least twice a week.
- Block out one hour a week for planning.
- Delegate one responsibility to a staff member.
- Start keeping a daily "to do" list.
- Only entertain staff problems if they have suggested solutions.
- Set monthly priorities and break them into managable tasks.
- Do up a weekly plan.
- Start tracking something you want to change, e.g. the hours you spend on telephone calls or in meetings.
- Stop taking work home.
- Schedule diary time to reset your monthly priorities.
- Delegate deadlines on longer term tasks.
- Schedule half an hour a week for "managing by wandering around".
- Schedule one hour a week to blitz paperwork, reading, etc.
- Redefine your role with your boss.
- Use discussion-enders with drop-ins.
- Hide for an hour a day or week.
- Work to the clock on big jobs.
- Start and finish all meetings on time.
- Record and time your telephone calls and plan to reduce them.

- Keep a time log over a couple of days.
- Get feedback on your bad time habits from your staff.
- Do important things in your peak energy hour.
- Block out two hours in the next month to think about the business.
- Tackle one thing on which you have been procrastinating.
- Have a daily nap or quiet time.
- Take half an hour's power walk in the evenings.
- Plan two events with family or friends this month.

Bring these commitments down onto your "to do" list, weekly planner or diary and when you have completed them choose another three until you start to see a difference. If you are having difficulty actioning any of the tasks consider breaking them into even smaller pieces or reflect on whether you really do want to change that particular piece of behaviour.

UNBLOCKING THE HABITS THAT KILL TIME

With the best of intentions many aspirations to change things in our lives come up against the force of habit, whether personal or organisational habits, sometimes called "culture". Start managing some of your bad habits by drawing up a list of the behaviours that get in the way of your personal effectiveness as a manager. It may help if you divide them into *personal* and *culture blocks*.

Personal	Culture
* Taking work home (A)	Long hours (A)
Not saying no (A)	Open door policy
* Poor time planning (A)	Instant response to customer queries
Over-commitment (A)	*Meetings scheduled at peak energy time (A)

Refine the list by asterisking (*) those which are the biggest blocks – it is better to work on the major blockages than those which have less influence on your effectiveness. Also identify the actionability of each (A). There is no point in trying to change things if you have no ability to influence them. Now plan to work on two of the big and actionable habits.

Break them into Bits

Treat your bad habits as baby elephants. You may not be able to tackle the whole problem but you could make a start on the easy bits. As part of the solution to poor time planning you could start with any of the following tasks.

- Keep a daily "to do" list.
- Redefine your major priorities with your boss.
- Establish regular Monday meetings with your staff.
- Block out diary time for projects.
- Review your major projects for half an hour each Monday morning.

Replace Bad Habits with Good Ones

Identify a good habit that may encourage you to let go of a bad habit. One of the best ways of reversing bad habits is to replace them with something else: for example, tackle the habit of working long hours by scheduling one night a week for the cinema, theatre or a meal.

The unfortunate thing about this world is that good habits are so much easier to give up than bad ones.

Somerset Maughan

Get Support for Your Good Habits

One of the reasons some people never attempt to give up smoking or lose weight is the overwhelming fear of failure. We often talk ourselves into failing before we start with language such as "I don't have a choice", "It's outside my control". Not only does negative dialogue tend to drain your energy but focusing on failure also blocks off the possibility of success.

Start building support for the habits you want to change by reversing the dialogue: "I will work less hours; I will plan my meetings better; I do have some control on my commitments." Also get support from others by telling your boss or staff what you intend to do differently and ask them to nag and reward you for going home on time, setting monthly priorities or reducing specific time wasters.

Persist a Little Longer

A research study that compared successful and less successful managers suggests one important difference is that successful managers keep going a little longer. Weight watchers claim that it takes up to 31 days to break the habits of a lifetime, so give yourself time to succeed. Make a commitment to doing one thing immediately, such as keeping a "to do" list or having some quiet time during the day, and commit to it for at least three weeks. If it is not working by then, try something else. Like most things in this life, there is no right answer to changing bad habits, just options that may or may not work in your particular circumstances. If you do not succeed with any of your existing options, resist the temptation to label yourself a failure; see it as a challenge to succeed by doing something else.

Managing time is not a set of handy hints for being better organised or speeding up the workflow – it is all too easy to be organised around the wrong things. Rather it is a process for making sure that you focus on the right things and put the time and energy where it belongs. And like most processes, it is a journey that requires direction, energy and perseverance.

Hopefully this book has given you some guidelines and challenged some of the habits that may be blocking you from achieving what you want as a manager. And the feeling that you are getting real mileage from all the effort you are putting into the job is the reward for good self-management – enjoy the journey.

ELEPHANTS & ANTS

Life is a journey, not a destination. Being more in control of your time also means getting a sense of balance into your work and personal life. Are there unfulfilled ambitions you could do something about in the next few months? Do you need or want to change anything about your job or life in the next month? Are there things you want to stop doing or give less time that you could make a start on this week?

Take more control of your time and yourself by focusing on what you want to achieve and dealing with the things that may be blocking you from what you want to get out of your job and your life – start to eat the elephants and fight the ants.

Birth is a beginning
And death a destination
And life a journey:
From childhood to maturity
And youth to age;
From innocence to awareness
And ignorance to knowing;
From foolishness to discretion and then,
Perhaps to Wisdom:
From weakness to strength
Or strength to weakness – and, often, back again;
From health to sickness and back, we pray,
to health again;
From offence to forgiveness,
From loneliness to love,
From joy to gratitude
From pain to compassion,
And grief to understanding – from fear to faith;
From defeat to defeat to defeat –
Until, looking backward or ahead,
We see that victory lies
Not at some high place along the way,
But in having made the journey, stage by stage.

(*Old Hebrew Prayer*)

Further Reading

P Drucker, *The Effective Executive* (London: Pan Books) 1970.

H J Freudenberger & G Richardson, *Burnout* (London: Arrow Books) 1985.

W J Knaus, *Do it Now: How to Stop Procrastinating* (New York: Prentice-Hall) 1979.

M Maltz, *Psycho-cybernetics* (Engelwood Cliffs: Wilshire Book Company) 1960.

M McCall & C A Segrist, *In Pursuit of the Manager's Job: Building on Mintzberg* (North Carolina, USA: Centre for Creative Leadership, Technical Report Number 14) 1980.

T McConalogue, "Real Delegation: The Art of Hanging On and Letting Go" *Management Decision* (1993) Vol. 31, No. 1, pp. 60-64.

T McConalogue, "Ten Tips for Time Management" *Management Magazine* (1996).

M McGannon, *The Urban Warriors Book of Solutions* (London: Pitman) 1996.

H Mintzberg, "The Managers Job: Folklore and Fact" *Harvard Business Review* (1975) 53,4.

W Oncken, *Managing Management Time* (New York: Prentice-Hall) 1984.

R G Rose, "Burnout" *Journal of Accountancy* (November 1986).

P Wilson, *Calm at Work* (London: Penguin Books) 1997.

For further information contact:

Tom McConalogue

Management and Organisation Development Consultant

32 Burlington Gardens

Dublin 4

Phone and Fax +353 (0)1 660 7312

E-mail mcconalt@clubi.ie